Contents

Part 1: Introduction   *page* 5
  Shakespeare's life   7
  Date of *Cymbeline*   9
  Sources   10
  The Elizabethan theatre   12
  A note on the text   16

Part 2: Summaries   18
  A general summary   18
  Detailed summaries   20

Part 3: Commentary   65
  Cymbeline and the 'last plays'   65
  The characters   71
  The language of *Cymbeline*   77

Part 4: Hints for study   87
  Methods of study   87
  Sample answers   91
  Practice questions   99

Part 5: Suggestions for further reading   101

The author of these notes   103

Part 1

Introduction

ENGLAND in the latter half of the sixteenth century was a small country ruled over by a virgin queen, Elizabeth I, whose main aim was to save her country from the dissension with which it had been plagued for more than a hundred years before her reign. The memory of the Wars of the Roses, in which claimants from the rival families of York and of Lancaster struggled to gain and hold the throne of England, still lingered in the minds of the people, and Shakespeare was to write at length on the subject of civil war and strife in his history plays, covering the period from the deposition of Richard II to the reign of Elizabeth's father, Henry VIII. England under Henry had become a Protestant country, with the monarch instead of the Pope as head of the Church, but many still held to the Catholic faith, and the fear of Catholic rebellion was still strong. The greatest event of Shakespeare's young manhood was the defeat in 1588 of the huge Armada which the Catholic Philip of Spain had despatched, with the blessing of the Pope, to conquer England and win it back for what he regarded as the true religion.

With this victory the country gained confidence in itself, but the cautious government still insisted on the need for obedience to the monarch and respect for the established order of society. Men were encouraged to look up to the Queen as an exalted figure embodying the ideals of chastity, justice and wisdom. Edmund Spenser (1552–99), the greatest Elizabethan poet before Shakespeare, wrote in his *Shepherd's Calendar* (1579):

> Of fair Elisa be your silver song,
>> That blessed wight,
> The flower of virgins: may she flourish long
>> In princely plight.

And Shakespeare's 'fair vestal, throned by the west' (*A Midsummer Night's Dream*, II.1.) is another of the countless tributes that were paid to Elizabeth in the literature of the time. While with shrewd political calculation she steered the country on a safe moderate course, the Queen surrounded herself with courtiers who praised her extravagantly, dressed brilliantly—as she herself did—and, though often intriguing for her hand in marriage, and the power which that would bring, kept up a pretence that the days of medieval chivalry, with its code of bravery and honour, were still alive.

Society was, however, changing. Men might be taught to know their place and keep within it, but the new economic forces favoured mobility. The medieval pattern of trade and manufacture conducted by 'guilds', which laid down conditions of, and restricted entry to, various businesses and professions, was giving way to the greater energy, and sometimes ruthlessness, of boldly enterprising individuals. The discovery of the New World changed men's geographical horizons, and though its riches were first exploited by the Spaniards, enmity between England and Spain gave excuse for men such as Sir Francis Drake (1540–96) and Sir Walter Raleigh (1552–1618) to carve a share for themselves as well, either by the thinly disguised piracy of Spanish ships, or by the colonisation of parts of America to which the Spaniards had not yet penetrated. Trade was extended eastwards as well, and Richard Hakluyt (1552–1616), in his *Principal Navigations, Voyages and Discoveries of the English Nation* (1589), was able to ask: 'Which of the kings of this land before her Majesty, had their banners ever seen in the Caspian Sea? Which of them hath ever dealt with the Emperor of Persia?' The intellectual discoveries of Copernicus (1473–1543) and Galileo (1564–1642), which were to revolutionise men's conception of the universe in which they lived, were as yet reaching only a few of the more intelligent and enquiring minds in Elizabethan England. The majority continued to think of the earth as fixed and stable, the centre of all things, round which the sun, moon and planets and stars moved in divinely ordained orbits. In other matters of learning, however, developments were taking place which were beginning to have more extensive effect. The universities had brought new scholarship to the study of the classical languages of Greece and Rome, new ideas were developing in medicine, mathematics and science, and the traditional view that man should concern himself only with knowledge that would help him to find his spiritual way to the next world was giving way, if only gradually, to an interest in knowledge that would enhance his understanding and enjoyment of life in this world.

Perhaps most important of all, the very nature of the English language was changing. Its grammar was being simplified and its vocabulary enormously increased by a flood of borrowings from foreign languages, especially Latin and Greek. A few purists objected, but the tide was irresistible. Writers soon gained confidence in the enhanced resources of the language and began to produce works which could challenge comparison with the best, both of the classical past and of more recent achievements in Italy and France. Sir Philip Sidney (1554–86) produced the elaborately decorative *Arcadia* (*c.*1580) and the sequence of love-sonnets, *Astrophel and Stella* (some time prior to 1586), in which he rivalled the famous Italian sonneteer, Petrarch (1304–74). Edmund Spenser, combining compliment to Queen Elizabeth with the epic grandeur of Vergil and the imaginative luxuriance of Ariosto (1474–1533) and Tasso (1544–95), wrote his long and complex poem, *The Faerie Queene*, the first three books of which appeared in 1590 and the rest in 1596. Both of these poets wrote for courtly and aristocratic readers. The popular art-form, which also appealed to all classes of society, was the drama. Through writers like John Lyly (1554–1606), George Peele (1558–97), Robert Greene (1560–92), Thomas Kyd (1557–97) and Christopher Marlowe (1564–93), this developed from the crude, ranting melodrama and knockabout farce of the mid-century interludes and plays into a subtle and expressive medium which could be used by Shakespeare to realise the possibilities of the flourishing English language to the full.

Shakespeare's life

William Shakespeare was born at Stratford-on-Avon in 1564. Tradition has it that the precise date of his birth was St George's Day, 23 April, but this may have arisen by confusion with the day of his death. The only exact record is that of his christening, 26 April, 1564. His father, John Shakespeare, was a businessman in Stratford, and prominent in local affairs until the late 1570s when, it seems, he fell into debt. His mother, Mary Arden, came from a higher social background, being the daughter of a gentleman and landowner, Robert Arden.

Little is known of Shakespeare's early life. He probably attended the Stratford school where he would have received a good grounding in Latin, and he may later have become a schoolmaster for a while. Stories about his having been apprenticed to a butcher (John Aubrey says that 'when he kill'd a calfe, he would doe it in a high style, and make a speech') and having stolen deer from the park of Sir Thomas Lucy of Charlecote, near Stratford, are without solid foundation. In November 1582 he married Anne Hathaway, of Shottery, a woman eight years older than himself, and their first daughter, Susanna, was christened on 26 May 1583. The dates suggest that Anne may have already been pregnant by him before they married, but since a contract may have been made prior to the church wedding, which in Elizabethan times would have been regarded as tantamount to marriage, there is no need to suppose, as some have done, that Shakespeare was reluctantly compelled to marry to save his child from the brand of bastardy. Two other children were born to Anne in 1585, the twins Hamnet and Judith, who were christened on 2 February. Both of the girls were later married to Stratford men, Susanna to John Hall, 5 June 1607, and Judith to Thomas Quiney, 10 February 1616; but the boy, Hamnet, only lived till he was eleven—his burial took place at Stratford on 11 August 1596.

For whatever reason—because he wanted to make his fortune, or because he had already been attracted to the profession of acting, or because he was compelled to leave Stratford under a cloud—some time in the late 1850s Shakespeare made his way without his family to London and became an actor-dramatist. He first joined the group of actors who enjoyed the protection of Lord Pembroke, and so were known as Lord Pembroke's Men, or Company, but later became a member of the Lord Chamberlain's Men, who, on the accession of James I to the throne of England, were honoured with the title of the King's Men. To begin with he was both actor and writer, his earliest plays being the history plays, *Henry VI*, Parts 1, 2 and 3, and *Richard III*; the tragedy of *Titus Andronicus*; and three comedies, *The Comedy of Errors*, *The Taming of the Shrew* and *The Two Gentlemen of Verona*. All of these were probably written by 1592, the year in which Robert Greene, one of the group of university-educated dramatists whose plays were popular when Shakespeare arrived in London, wrote maliciously on his death-bed, urging his friends not to trust the players any longer, 'for there is an upstart Crow, beautified with our feathers, that with his *Tygers hart wrapt in a Players hyde*, supposes he is as well able to bombast out a blanke verse as the best of you: and beeing an absolute *Iohannes fac totum* [Johnny-do-all], is in his owne conceit the onely Shake-scene in a countrey.' (*Greenes Groats-worth of Wit*, 1592.) This is clearly a jealous reference to Shakespeare (it parodies the line from Part 3 of *Henry VI*, I.4.137, in which York addresses the fierce virago, Queen Margaret, as 'O tiger's heart wrapp'd in a woman's hide'), and suggests that he had already by 1592 established himself as one of the leading men in the theatre of his day.

Tradition has it that among Shakespeare's roles as an actor were Adam in *As You Like It* (1599) and the ghost in *Hamlet* (1600-1). These are minor parts, and though he may have taken some major roles as well (one of his contemporaries says that he was an excellent actor), he became so busy as a playwright that most of his time must have been occupied in composition. In the 1590s he wrote seven more comedies besides those already mentioned, culminating in *Twelfth Night* (1599-1600); four more history plays; two more tragedies, and two narrative poems, *Venus and Adonis* and *The Rape of Lucrece*; and the bulk of the Sonnets (though they were not published till 1609). At the beginning of the new century tragedy began to occupy him almost completely, and he wrote a series of plays which are the most passionate and profound that England has ever known: *Hamlet*, *Othello* (1604-5), *Macbeth* (1605-6), *King Lear* (1605-6) and *Antony and Cleopatra* (1606-7).

During the whole of this period Shakespeare lived and worked in London, occupying lodgings not far from the theatres on which his life was centred; but he did not forget Stratford. The claim to a coat of arms, the sign of a man's status as a gentleman, which his father tried unsuccessfully to secure for his family, was taken up again and achieved by Shakespeare in 1596. In the following year he bought a substantial house in Stratford called New Place, and he acquired other property in 1602. From time to time he made return visits to his native town, and from about 1610 he made it his home once more. Shakespeare continued, however, to write plays and to visit London. The so-called 'last plays' (*Pericles, Cymbeline, The Winter's Tale* and *The Tempest*) belong to the years from 1608–12, and—though it is dangerous to try to infer Shakespeare's state of mind from interpretation of his work—indicate a certain mellowing of outlook and a preoccupation with the relations between parents and children which seem to suggest a man who is beginning to take stock of the past and think of the future in terms of the handing on of life to the next generation. His final play was *Henry VIII*, written in collaboration with John Fletcher, 1613. This was also the year in which the Globe theatre was destroyed by fire.

Early in January 1616 Shakespeare made his will. Bequests were made to Stratford acquaintances and to his actor-friends, Richard Burbage (1567–1619), John Heminges (d.1630) and Henry Condell (d.1627) (the latter pair became, after his death, the editors of the first complete edition of Shakespeare's works, the First Folio of 1623), but the major part of his estate was made over to his family. He died on 23 April 1616.

Date of *Cymbeline*

In Simon Forman's *Booke of Plaies*, a record of performances seen by Forman at the Globe Theatre at the beginning of the seventeenth century, there is an account headed, 'Of Cimbalin king of England' (see *A Short Life of Shakespeare* by E. K. Chambers, abridged by Charles Williams, Oxford University Press, Oxford, 1933, p.182). No date is given for this, but it is preceded by an account of 'Mackbeth' which is dated 20 April 1610 (by the modern calendar this would be 1611). The likelihood is that *Cymbeline* was seen at much the same time. There are certain resemblances between *Cymbeline* and Beaumont and Fletcher's *Philaster*, a play which was in existence before October 1610, and if, as now seems likely (see J. M. Nosworthy's discussion of the relationship between the two plays, Arden edition, Methuen, London, 1955, pp.xxxvii–xl), *Philaster* was an imitation of *Cymbeline*, rather than the other way about, this would suggest a date for *Cymbeline* not later than 1610. For reasons given in Part 3 of these Notes it clearly belongs to the group of Shakespeare's plays comprising *Pericles, The Winter's Tale* and *The Tempest*, normally dated 1608–12, and since, on stylistic grounds, it is likely that *Cymbeline* follows *Pericles* and precedes *The Winter's Tale*, it is reasonable to assume a date of 1608–10 for

Cymbeline. Nosworthy and Maxwell (*The New Cambridge Shakespeare*, Cambridge University Press, Cambridge, 1960, p.xii) narrow this down to 1609–10. Given the vagueness of the evidence, this is probably as precise a date as can be fixed.

Sources

There is no single source for the whole of *Cymbeline.* Shakespeare has taken different stories from different sources and combined them together for his own purposes.

The main source for the wager story is II.9 of the *Decameron* (1358) by the Italian writer Boccaccio (1313–75) (an English translation of 1620 is reprinted in Bullough's *Narrative and Dramatic Sources of Shakespeare*, Routledge and Kegan Paul, London, 1975, vol. 8, pp.50–63). This tells how a merchant, Bernado Lomellino, engages in a bet with Ambrogiuolo on the virtue of his (Bernado's) wife, Genevra. To win the bet Ambrogiuolo persuades a poor woman-friend of Genevra's to let him hide in a chest, which she asks Genevra to keep in her own chamber for two or three days. He comes out of the chest at night, notes the circumstances of the chamber and the presence of a small wart on her left breast with yellow hairs growing upon it, and steals a ring, a purse, a dress and a girdle. Later he uses these to make Bernado believe that Genevra has been false, the wart being the finally convincing detail. Bernado orders a servant to kill her, but Genevra persuades the servant to allow her to escape in man's apparel. Thereafter, in a sequence of events very different from Shakespeare's, Genevra, adopting the name of Sicurano da Finale, becomes the favourite of the Soldan, and uses her position to bring Bernado and Ambrogiuolo together in a public confrontation, the outcome of which is the exposure of Ambrogiuolo's deception and the revelation of Sicurano's true identity. Genevra and Bernado are reunited, but Ambrogiuolo is impaled on a stake, 'annointed with honey' and 'devoured to the bare bones, by Flies, Waspes, and Hornets' (Bullough, ibid., vol. 8, p.62).

Another version of this story is *Frederyke of Jennen* (i.e. Genoa), printed in English in 1518, but translated from the Dutch (the text of the 1560 edition is reprinted in Bullough, ibid., vol. 8, pp.63–78). Shakespeare probably knew both versions, as there are certain details to be found in the *Decameron* and *Cymbeline*, but not in *Frederyke of Jennen*, and likewise details in *Frederyke* and *Cymbeline* not in the *Decameron*. In *Frederyke*, for example, it is Johan of Florence (the equivalent of Ambrogiuolo) who initiates the bet, as Iachimo does in *Cymbeline*. Neither version contains any preliminary attempt at seduction similar to Iachimo's lying about Posthumus's behaviour in Rome, but *Frederyke* is the nearer of the two in that Johan on encountering Ambrose's

(= Bernado's) wife finds her of such 'womanly behavoure' that 'he was a shamed and sayd to hym selfe: "Alas, poore wretche that I am, what have I done? The money is lost, I se it wel. For she semeth a worshypfull woman and I dare not speke of that vylany, whereof I am sory."' (Bullough, ibid., p.66). This perhaps gave Shakespeare the cue for Iachimo's overawed reaction on first meeting Imogen (I.5). On the other hand, Imogen's 'mole cinque-spotted, like the crimson drops/I' th' bottom of a cowslip' (II.2) is much closer to Genevra's 'small wart upon her left pappe, with some few haires growing thereon, appearing to be as yellow as gold' (Bullough, ibid., p. 55) than to the 'blacke warte' on the arm of Ambrose's wife (Bullough, ibid., p.69).

The sequel in *Frederyke* departs even more from the subsequent events in *Cymbeline* than the sequel in the *Decameron*. Ambrose's wife, disguised as Frederyke (hence the title in this version), becomes, most improbably, the trusted governor of the King of Alkare, and successfully defends his kingdom from attack. Ambrose is eventually reconciled with his wife, and Johan is executed; but in neither source is there the general forgiveness of *Cymbeline* which includes both deceived and deceiver.

The pseudo-historical material of *Cymbeline* and the tribute issue is derived from Raphael Holinshed's (*d. c.*1580) *Historie of England* (1587 edition)—the source used by Shakespeare for his history plays. According to Holinshed, however, it was Cymbeline's successor, Guiderius, who brought war to Britain by refusing to pay the tribute to Rome. Other versions were probably known to Shakespeare, including material added in 1587 by Thomas Blennerhasset and John Higgins to *The Mirror for Magistrates* (originally published 1559) and Spenser's *The Faerie Queene* (Books I–III, published 1589), II.10.50–1, which identifies Cymbeline as the one who denied tribute (see Arden edition of *Cymbeline*, xvii–xix and 212–16).

Holinshed is also the source for the stand made by Belarius, Guiderius, Arviragus and the disguised Posthumus in the narrow lane, which turns imminent defeat into victory. This material comes, however, from that part of Holinshed's *Historie* which is devoted to Scotland and has nothing to do with Cymbeline. The original of Belarius is a farmer called Haie. With the help of two of his sons he intervenes in the battle between the Scots, under King Kenneth, and the Danes, thus helping King Kenneth to rally his troops.

An anonymous romance-play called *The Rare Triumphes of Love and Fortune* (printed 1589) may also have provided Shakespeare with further suggestions for *Cymbeline*. It offers a parallel to the Imogen–Posthumus love story in 'the love of Princess Fidelia for the seeming orphan Hermione, who has been brought up at the Court by her father, King Phizantius' (Arden edition, p.xxv); and the banished courtier, Bomelio, may have provided material which Shakespeare combined with the

Scottish farmer, Haie, from Holinshed, to round out the character of
Belarius. Richard Hosley (editor of the Signet edition of *Cymbeline*,
New American Library, New York, 1968) suggests that Shakespeare
combined the material derived from this play with 'the folk-tale motif of
the Wicked Stepmother', and that Imogen's stay with Belarius,
Guiderius and Arviragus in the Welsh mountains, disguised as Fidele,
may owe something to the pastoral episode of Torquato Tasso's
Jerusalem Delivered (1576), VII (Signet edition, pp.xxv–xxvi). The
latter, however, is part of a pastoral tradition which was so much a
feature of the Elizabethan literary inheritance that Shakespeare could
have derived it from anywhere. Ultimately, it may be traced back to the
pastoral interludes in late Greek romances, such as the *Daphnis and
Chloe* of Longus and the *Aethiopian History* of Heliodorus (both from
about the second century AD), which, through their recurrent theme of
separation and reunion, may also, as Hosley says, have influenced
Cymbeline. (See Signet edition, xxx–xxxi. For a more detailed account of
Greek romances and their relationship to Elizabethan literature, and to
Shakespeare, in particular, see S. L. Wolff: *Greek Romances in
Elizabethan Prose Fiction*, Columbia University Press, Newton, 1912,
and Edwin Greenlaw: *Shakespeare's Pastorals, Studies in Philology*, vol.
13, no. 2, University of North Carolina, Durham, North Carolina,
1916.)

The source material for *Cymbeline* is thus complex and uncertain.
How much Shakespeare took from any one story or play cannot be
stated with confidence, and even which particular works were the
sources that he consulted is subject to debate. What is clear, however, is
that he took hints from a wide range of sources, and combined them
ingeniously to form the interwoven plot of *Cymbeline*. He borrowed
extensively, perhaps, but he made those borrowings his own. The play
which he created out of them echoes and re-echoes with pseudo-history,
and more especially with the time-honoured motifs of romance literature, but it constitutes an essentially original creation.

The Elizabethan theatre

The circumstances in which Shakespeare's plays were originally seen by
Elizabethan audiences were very different from those in which we see
them in present-day theatres. The Elizabethan stage was essentially a
raised platform, some 28ft long, and from 24ft to 43ft wide, protruding
into an open yard surrounded by wooden galleries. Trap-doors were set
into the floor of the stage, through which devils, fairies and other
supernatural beings could make their exits and entrances, if so needed;
or if deities were required to descend from heaven (as Jupiter does,
'sitting upon an eagle', in *Cymbeline*, V.4), they could be let down from

another trap-door in the short roof which covered the platform. At the back of the main stage was a smaller recess, or inner-stage, known as the 'study', which could be curtained off from the view of the audience. This might be used to represent such places as Imogen's bedchamber, or Belarius's cave (in *Cymbeline*), or Prospero's cell (in Shakespeare's *The Tempest*). Above it would be a balcony (the 'chamber'), suitable for the scene in Shakespeare's *Romeo and Juliet* where Juliet enters 'above at a window' and speaks to Romeo below in the 'orchard' (*Romeo and Juliet*, II.2). Above this again would be the 'music gallery', where the music, which was an integral part of Elizabethan drama, would be played.

The Elizabethan theatre derived its basic shape from the old English

THE GLOBE PLAYHOUSE

The theatre, originally built by James Burbage in 1576, was made of wood (Burbage had been trained as a carpenter). It was situated to the north of the River Thames on Shoreditch in Finsbury Fields. There was trouble with the lease of the land, and so the theatre was dismantled in 1598, and reconstructed 'in another forme' on the south side of the Thames as the Globe. Its sign is thought to have been a figure of the Greek hero Hercules carrying the globe. It was built in six months, its galleries being roofed with thatch. This caught fire in 1613 when some smouldering wadding, from a cannon used in a performance of Shakespeare's *Henry VIII*, lodged in it. The theatre was burnt down, and when it was rebuilt again on the old foundations, the galleries were roofed with tiles.

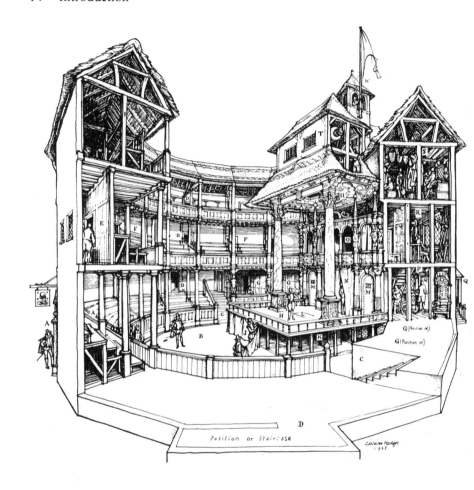

A CONJECTURAL RECONSTRUCTION OF THE INTERIOR OF
THE GLOBE PLAYHOUSE

AA Main entrance
 B The Yard
CC Entrances to lowest gallery
 D Entrance to staircase and upper galleries
 E Corridor serving the different sections of the
   middle gallery
 F Middle gallery ('Twopenny Rooms')
 G 'Gentlemen's Rooms' or Lords' Rooms'
 H The stage
 J The hanging being put up round the stage
 K The 'Hell' under the stage
 L The stage trap, leading down to the Hell
MM Stage doors

 N Curtained 'place behind the stage'
 O Gallery above the stage, used as required
   sometimes by musicians, sometimes by
   spectators, and often as part of the play
 P Back-stage area (the tiring-house)
 Q Tiring-house door
 R Dressing-rooms
 S Wardrobe and storage
 T The hut housing the machine for lowering
   enthroned gods, etc., to the stage
 U The 'Heavens'
 W Hoisting the playhouse flag

inns, which were built round an enclosed courtyard. It was at such inns that performances most frequently took place prior to the building of London's new public theatres, and inns continued throughout Shakespeare's life to be the usual places of performance in country towns. The first of the new theatres, called 'The Theater', was built in 1576 on the south bank of the Thames by James Burbage, father of Richard Burbage, later to become the first great Shakespearean actor. This was soon followed by other theatres such as the Curtain, Hope, Rose, Fortune and Globe. Among these the Fortune was square-shaped, the Globe octagonal, or, in a general sense, round (hence the reference in the Prologue of Shakespeare's history play, *Henry V*, to 'this wooden O'). Built in part from the materials of the dismantled Theater, and opened in 1599, the Globe was to become the most famous of all Elizabethan theatres as the home of the Lord Chamberlain's men, the company of players which Shakespeare himself joined in 1594, and hence the major site for the production of all his plays from 1599 onwards.

All these theatres were open to the sky. Only the galleries, where the better-off spectators sat, and the stage itself were roofed. Ordinary playgoers stood for a penny each in the uncovered yard surrounding the stage and took their chance with the weather. Noblemen who wished to see the play were accommodated, at a higher price, in those parts of the galleries which were nearest the stage, but partitioned off from the rest of the theatre, while the 'gallants' (young men who prided themselves on their wit and fashion) paid for the privilege of sitting on the stage as conspicuous to the whole audience as the actors themselves.

Certain indoor theatres were built in the early seventeenth century, and it may have been at one of these, the Blackfriars, that *Cymbeline* was first performed. But it would almost certainly have been presented at the Globe as well. It was with the open-air theatre in mind that Shakespeare wrote most of his work, and, above all, it was the open-air theatre which shaped his ideas of dramatic art. There performances took place in the afternoon by daylight. The artificial illumination, and consequently elaborate lighting effects, of the modern theatre were unavailable, and there was little scope for the elaborate scene-setting which is made possible in the modern theatre by the combination of lighting and sophisticated stage machinery and by marking off the edge of the stage with a line of the footlights instead of allowing it to protrude into the middle of the audience. Some simple stage properties were used, but most scenic effects, together with indications of place and the sense of the passing of time, were created through words. The absence of realistic settings, and the willingness of audiences to let their imaginations be acted upon by the poetic resources of language, were essential conditions of Elizabethan dramatic practice. What might have seemed a disadvantage was turned into a great asset, for the minds of the audience went wherever the actors' words directed them. There was no need for elaborate changes of scenery: one group of actors simply left the stage and another group came on immediately after them, indicating, if necessary, through their speeches where they were and what they were doing. The result was great speed and fluidity of action, making it quite credible, as is claimed in the prologue to *Romeo and Juliet*, that the performance of a play would be but 'the two hours' traffic of our stage'.

The relationship between actor and audience must also have been more intimate than in a modern theatre (except where this is deliberately encouraged, as, for example, in the twentieth century 'theatre in the round', which uses a centrally placed stage surrounded by the audience on all sides). By advancing to the forward part of the stage the actor could speak an 'aside' to the audience as if taking them into his confidence, and deliver a soliloquy (a speech in which a character alone on the stage speaks out his thought aloud, or frankly gives information to the audience) without seeming unnatural and absurd as he would be inclined to do in the modern theatre. The Elizabethans, of course, were no more disposed than modern audiences to believe in asides or soliloquies as true to life. On the contrary, they were fully aware of such dramatic conventions, which they accepted as customs of theatrical presentation and convenient ways of making a certain kind of communication possible between actor and audience. A striking example is Oberon (King of the Fairies in Shakespeare's *A Midsummer Night's Dream*) who becomes invisible to the other characters on stage by merely saying 'I am invisible'. He need make no clumsy attempts to hide himself; the members of the audience simply accept the convention that, although they can see him quite clearly, the mortal characters within the play cannot. The convention of stage-disguise is equally simple, and equally effective, whether it concerns Rosalind, the heroine of Shakespeare's *As You Like It*, who, when dressed up as the boy Ganymede is unrecognisable even to her own father, or Imogen dressed as Fidele, who goes unrecognised by the entire court till Pisanio steps forward with his 'How fares my mistress' (*Cymbeline*, V.5). Such conventions were the rules of the Elizabethan dramatic game with which the audience were quite familiar, and which they tacitly accepted when entering the theatre.

The style of acting adopted in the Elizabethan theatre may also have been much more conventional than that of the modern theatre. A modern actor is trained to think himself into the mind of the character he is acting and to adopt the tone of voice and gestures which he thinks such a character would use if he existed as an actual person. Careful choice of appropriate dress and realistic make-up complete this elaborate pretence. An Elizabethan actor was also dressed with great care, though not necessarily in a way that would seem appropriate by modern standards. But the purpose of the actor—whatever the nature of his part—would have been above all else to deliver his words in a resounding voice capable of doing justice to their poetic expressiveness. The language would come first, and the representation of character second. With such an approach to acting it would not, of course, seem odd that the imaginary personages on the stage should speak in verse, which, especially in Shakespeare's earlier comedies, was often intricately rhymed, and that they should from time to time break into song. This, too, was a convention gladly accepted by the audience for the heightening of their own enjoyment of the play.

If a modern equivalent is sought for it is more likely to be found in the production of opera, or 'musical comedy', than in the so-called 'straight theatre'. A performance of *Cymbeline*, in particular, should be approached in the spirit of opera rather than realism. It is almost to be regretted that it is not among those Shakespeare plays which the Italian composer Giuseppe Verdi (1813–1901) turned into music drama. The action of the play, especially in the last scene, which seems so preposterous to a modern audience, would seem less absurd in the context of opera—or, to adapt the words of the gravedigger in Shakespeare's *Hamlet*, 'if 'a do not, 'tis no great matter there . . .' Twill not be seen in him there: there the men are as mad as he' (*Hamlet*, V.1.147–50). On a more serious level, the play itself is a symbolic drama. Its purpose is to show discord finally resolved into a harmony which is explained for us by the significantly named 'Philarmonus' (lover of harmony), and it is interpreted by him, in appropriately musical imagery, as the work of the gods:

> The fingers of the pow'rs above do tune
> The harmony of this peace.   (V.5.464–5)

Thus the action breaks out of the frame of an imitation of real life, and becomes a matter essentially of convention—an orchestration of speeches and actions by means of which the hidden justice and benevolence of the divine powers is revealed to us.

A note on the text

Cymbeline was first printed in the Folio edition of Shakespeare's plays edited after his death by his fellow-members of the King's Men, John Heminge and Henry Condell. They called it *The Tragedie of Cymbeline* and placed it at the end of the First Folio. The text is a good one and may have been taken from a scribe's copy of Shakespeare's manuscript.

The text of *Cymbeline* to which references are made in these Notes is that to be found in *The Alexander Edition of William Shakespeare, The Complete Works*, edited by Peter Alexander, Collins, London and Glasgow, 1951.

Part 2

Summaries
of CYMBELINE

A general summary

The plot of *Cymbeline* is composed of the interweaving of four separate strands: (1) the wager-plot, involving Imogen, Posthumus and Iachimo; (2) the Queen's conspiracy to wrest control of Britain from Cymbeline and ensure the throne for her son, Cloten; (3) the story of Belarius's abduction of Guiderius and Arviragus; and (4) the dispute over tribute between Britain and Rome.

Cymbeline himself, though a somewhat lifeless character, provides a unifying link between these four plot elements. It is he who opposes Imogen's marriage to Posthumus, and, by banishing the latter to Italy, brings about the separation which is essential for the wager. It is his unmanly submission to his second wife, the Queen (mother, by a previous marriage, of Cloten, and step-mother of Imogen), which makes her conspiracy possible; and it was his irrational anger against the faithful Belarius which, at the time when Guiderius and Arviragus were children, led to Belarius's act of revenge by kidnapping. As King of Britain he is also one of the principal characters involved in the dispute with Rome. Under the influence of the Queen he withholds the tribute promised by his uncle, Cassibelan, to Julius Caesar, and so brings about the Roman invasion of Britain.

Unity is also effected, however, by the intermingling of characters from one plot area with characters from other areas, and by the impact of events related to one area on those related to others. The wager made by Posthumus on the chastity of Imogen brings Iachimo on his first visit to Britain. Iachimo's deception of Posthumus by means of the trunk trick leads to Posthumus's unfounded jealousy, and this in its turn to the false letter to Imogen which sets her on the way to Milford Haven, and to the order that Pisanio shall use this opportunity to kill her.

The Queen's encouragement of Cloten's suit to Imogen, by which she hopes to place her son on the throne of Britain, brings the rebuff which so enrages Cloten that he extorts a 'confession' from Pisanio, and on the basis of that he dresses himself in Posthumus's clothes with the intention of pursuing her to Milford, killing Posthumus, and raping her. Both Imogen and Cloten are thus directed to the mountainous region where Belarius lives with the abducted sons of Cymbeline, who take him for their father. Imogen, disguised as the boy, Fidele, finds shelter with her unknown brothers; but the influence of the Queen still pursues her, not only in the shape of Cloten—leading to Cloten's death at the hands of Guiderius—but also in the form of the potion given by the Queen to Pisanio, and passed on by him to Imogen in the belief that it is a sovereign remedy. The Queen had believed it to be fatal, but she herself was deceived by her physician, Cornelius, who, mistrusting her intentions, gave her a drug calculated to produce only the semblance of death. Imogen now swallows it, with the result that she appears dead to Belarius, Guiderius and Arviragus. They grieve over her, and then lay her by the side of Cloten's headless corpse, which is still clad in Posthumus's clothes. On waking, Imogen thinks the body to be that of Posthumus, and believes herself to be the victim of a conspiracy between Pisanio and Cloten.

The appearance at this very moment of Lucius and the Romans, who have just landed at Milford, inspires Imogen to offer her services as a page to the Roman commander. Meanwhile, Posthumus and Iachimo are both introduced to the Romano-British area of the plot by the inclusion of the Italian gentry into the Roman forces. Posthumus, however, full of remorse since he believes himself guilty of Imogen's murder, and ready to die, disguises himself as a British peasant in order to fight on the British side. In so doing he leagues himself with the three strangers (Belarius, Guiderius and Arviragus) who have also joined the British forces, and who by their valour turn a British rout into unexpected victory. Afterwards Posthumus, reverting to his 'Roman' identity, deliberately surrenders himself to Cymbeline, and calmly accepts the sentence of death passed on all the invading forces.

In the elaborate dénouement of the play's final scene all areas come together, and, with the exception of Cloten, already slain, and the Queen, whose death-bed confession is reported by Cornelius, all the chief characters appear on stage. By a sequence of astonishing revelations all the characters are made known to each other, and all the mysteries of the story cleared up: the plot of the Queen is exposed; the nature of Iachimo's deception of Posthumus is explained, and Imogen and Posthumus are reunited; Cloten's death is announced, and with it the identity of his killer—bringing in its train the restoration of Guiderius and Arviragus to their true father; and, finally, the Romans are reprieved, the payment of tribute is renewed, and peace between Britain and Rome is established once more.

Detailed summaries

Act I Scene 1

Two gentlemen of the court of Cymbeline, King of Britain, discuss the latest news. Imogen (the King's daughter by his first wife), whom Cymbeline wished to marry to Cloten (the only son of his second wife), has given her hand, instead, to Posthumus Leonatus. Enraged at this, the King has imprisoned Imogen and banished Posthumus. The courtiers, however, though appearing to agree with the King, secretly approve the marriage. According to the First Gentleman, Cloten is utterly unworthy of Imogen, whereas Posthumus is a paragon of virtue. The First Gentleman explains that Posthumus was born soon after the death of his father, Sicilius Leonatus, a soldier who fought with Cassibelan against the Romans, and that his mother died in childbirth: hence the name, Posthumus (= after death). Cymbeline brought him up at court, where he was admired by everybody. The First Gentleman also says that Cymbeline originally had two sons, but that they were abducted from their nursery and that nothing has been heard of them since. The Queen enters, with Posthumus and Imogen. She has been appointed Imogen's gaoler, but professes to be a friend of them both, and allows them to talk privately together for a while. But Imogen is not deceived; she knows that the Queen hates her. Imogen and Posthumus say farewell to each other, and exchange a ring and a bracelet as tokens of their mutual love. The Queen, meanwhile, has betrayed them by bringing the King to see their forbidden meeting. Posthumus is angrily dismissed; but Imogen speaks out boldly for him. At the end of the scene Pisanio, the trusted servant of Posthumus, reports a futile attempt by Cloten to fight with Posthumus. Pisanio himself has been sent by Posthumus to carry out whatever commands Imogen may give him.

The purpose of this introductory scene is frankly informative. A modern realistic dramatist would probably seek to convey the necessary information about what has happened before the play begins in a more plausible manner; but Shakespeare, in common with most of the Elizabethans, does not worry unduly about creating the illusion of actual conversation. He tackles the problem of exposition in a straightforward way, and tells the audience what they need to know. For this, in effect, is what the First Gentleman is doing. He is ostensibly bringing the Second Gentleman up to date with affairs at the court; but he is really imparting basic information to the audience without which the play could not go forward. It is the dramatic equivalent of the storyteller's 'Once upon a time ...', and has the additional merit of being clearer and more economical than the realist's often tortuous devices for giving information without appearing to do so.

Shakespeare's skill, however, is shown in the way in which he combines exposition with characterisation and, especially in *Cymbeline*, with thematic material. By the end of this scene the audience is aware not only of the basic situation, but of the characters of Posthumus, Imogen, Cymbeline, the Queen and Cloten. But just as the exposition makes no pretence to realism, so the characterisation is boldly simplified rather than psychologically complex. This, too, has something of a fairy-story quality. Posthumus, described at length in the First Gentleman's speech in lines 28–54, is the noble hero. He is above all a man of honour, a true gentleman—which is why so much attention is given to his ancestry. Yet he has no titles, and it is significant that the First Gentleman calls him 'a poor but worthy gentleman' (line 7). He represents innate worth rather than social position—in sharp contrast to Cloten, who, though the Queen's son, is 'a thing/ Too bad for bad report' (lines 16–17). The contrast is reinforced by brief reference to an abortive fight between them (lines 159–66). Posthumus does not take Cloten's affront seriously, otherwise the outcome would have been much worse for Cloten. We already sense that the latter is ill-mannered and a coward, characteristics which are fully revealed as the plot develops.

The Queen likewise already emerges as two-faced and treacherous. She has much in common with the fairy-tale witch, or wicked stepmother, and her very first words are a negative definition of this. What she denies herself to be is by that very means inserted into the minds of the audience as a significant clue to what she actually is:

No, be assur'd you shall not find me, daughter,
After the slander of most stepmothers,
Evil-ey'd unto you.

(lines 70–2)

Imogen, however, is not deceived; and the Queen's action in bringing Cymbeline to see the meeting between Imogen and Posthumus confirms the audience's impression that what Imogen says is right.

Imogen is the antithesis of the Queen, just as Posthumus is the antithesis of Cloten. Unlike the Queen, she is direct and honest. At the same time she gives respect and obedience where it is due. Thus, her attitude towards her father's disapproval of Posthumus is compounded of both defiance and submission. She trusts her own judgement—and we trust hers, partly because we see that the First Gentleman values her judgement and regards her 'election' (line 53) of Posthumus as the surest sign that Posthumus has intrinsic worth. Moreover, she can stand up to her father's anger with admirable courage. But, like Cordelia in Shakespeare's *King Lear*, who also disobeys her father without forfeiting the audience's regard, she retains an essential respect for Cymbeline's kingly and paternal authority. The integration of these two

seemingly contradictory attitudes is expressed in her words to
Posthumus:

> My dearest husband,
> I something fear my father's wrath, but nothing—
> Always reserved my holy duty—what
> His rage can do on me.

(lines 85–8)

Her 'holy duty' (compare Cordelia's 'bond') is the sacred respect which
the child should have for the father, and this she retains even while she
asserts that she is not afraid of the consequences which his anger might
have for her. Imogen has a proper reverence for her father's displeasure,
but she lacks the merely cowardly fear, or the fear that comes from self-
distrust.

This mixture of respect and defiance in Imogen's attitude towards her
father raises the question of Order. The conflict arises because
Cymbeline himself is not the perfect embodiment of order which, as
King, he should be. He has let himself fall under the influence of the
Queen, who can boast that she never does him wrong without making
him pay to be friends with her again (lines 104–5). She has an emotional
hold over him which warps his judgement. There is a sense of
disharmony in the land which emanates from the King. This is conveyed
by the very first lines of the play:

> You do not meet a man but frowns; our bloods
> No more obey the heavens than our courtiers
> Still seem as does the King's.

(lines 1–3)

That is, the mood of the courtiers reflects that of the King, just as 'our
bloods' depend on the influence of the stars (astrology was taken much
more seriously in the seventeenth than it is in the twentieth century); and
since the King is troubled, so are those surrounding him. Corruption in
the King affects the whole court.

As we have seen, the courtiers do not accept the ill-judgement of the
King with regard to Imogen's choice of Posthumus. They only appear to
agree with him:

> But not a courtier,
> Although they wear their faces to the bent
> Of the King's looks, hath a heart that is not
> Glad at the thing they scowl at.

(lines 12–14)

Nevertheless, this split between appearance and reality is a sign of
disorder. It is an unhealthy situation for Britain, one which the Queen

can exploit for her evil purposes. She herself cultivates false appearance in a more dangerous form, as we see in her hypocrisy towards Imogen and Posthumus. She makes a pretence of peace-making, but in reality exacerbates trouble.

The opening scene thus points towards a growingly tragic situation: disorder, appearance divided from reality, the King in an ill-judged rage against his own offspring. But there are also suggestions, though their significance is not apparent to the audience at this early point in the play, of the existence of counterbalancing forces. We hear, for example, of the lost sons (lines 57–67) who will enter the play later, and Imogen's touch of pastoral wishful-thinking (lines 148–50) anticipates the pastoral setting in which those sons will be introduced to us (in Act III Scene 3). Moreover, there is a note of comedy in the account of the abduction of the sons which seems to accord rather oddly with the theme of their loss:

> 2 GENT.   That a king's children should be so convey'd,
> So slackly guarded, and the search so slow
> That could not trace them!
> 1 GENT.   Howsoe'er 'tis strange,
> Or that the negligence may well be laugh'd at,
> Yet it is true, sir.

(lines 63–7)

The text itself draws attention to the elements of the incredible and the ridiculous in this disappearance, and though it may well be that the rest of the scene, with its passionate and tragic intensity, overwhelms this slight touch of the absurd, a note has been struck which modifies the prevailing tragic tone, and can later be seen in retrospect as a hint that the play belongs to the realm of tragi-comedy rather than tragedy proper.

NOTES AND GLOSSARY:

bloods: emotions, temperament. The First Gentleman says that courtiers fit their mood to the King's just as our temperaments are influenced by the heavens
admir'd: causing wonder
the sur-addition Leonatus: the additional name, 'Leonatus' (= lion-born)
fond of issue: doting on his offspring
Posthumus: born after the father's death
election: choice
slander of most stepmothers: that which is slanderously said of most stepmothers
Can tickle where she wounds: the Queen can seem to please when she is really hurting

fear:	respect, hold in awe. In lines 85–8 Shakespeare plays on two senses of the word 'fear': fear as cowardice, which Imogen denies, and fear in this sense of respect. In the latter sense it is similar to 'the fear of the Lord' which in the Bible is said to be 'the beginning of wisdom' (*Psalms* 111:10)
cere up:	wrap up in a shroud; possibly also seal (compare 'bonds of death', line 117)
puttock:	kite (hawk, bird of prey). Inferior to the 'eagle', (line 139). Posthumus is the 'eagle', Cloten the 'puttock'

Act I Scene 2

Cloten discusses his recent encounter with Posthumus, one courtier flattering him, the other in asides (words spoken to the audience which are, by convention, not audible to the other characters on stage) revealing how little Cloten has actually done. Cloten professes to regret that no blood was drawn, but it is clear that this was merely the result of Posthumus's refusal to be provoked.

This brief scene serves mainly to underline the impression already created that Cloten is a fool and an empty boaster. The dialogue, typical of Shakespearean humour, is full of puns which enable the Lords to gibe at Cloten while they appear to be praising him.

NOTES AND GLOSSARY:

His body's a passable carcass:	the First Lord says that Posthumus's body has been run through many times by Cloten's sword thrusts ('passes'), and that it is a tolerable carcass. He thus flatters and mocks Cloten simultaneously
His steel was in debt; it went o' th' back side the town:	a mocking comment on Cloten's swordsmanship. It means that Cloten was in reality so cowardly that he kept his sword from making contact with Posthumus's like a debtor sneaking through side-streets to avoid his creditors
inches:	islands (but also modern 'inches')
If it be a sin to make a true election, she is damn'd:	a pun on the theological sense of 'election' meaning 'predetermined by God to salvation', and 'election' meaning 'choice'

Act I Scene 3

Pisanio gives Imogen an account of Posthumus's departure. Imogen insists that she would have watched his ship until it disappeared; she regrets that there was not time to tell him all the things that she would have wished.

This is another brief scene, but it does not imply new scene-setting. As explained in Part 1, one group of actors enters as soon as another group leaves. Thus, at the end of Act I Scene 2, Cloten invites the two courtiers with whom he has been speaking to go with him to his chamber, a clear indication that they walk off through one of the exits at the back of the stage. Even while they are still going, Imogen and Pisanio can be seen coming on to the stage from another entrance, and their speech almost overlaps with that of Cloten and his followers. The result is a rapid, unbroken flow of action.

What we have here is a touching love scene with only one of the pair of lovers present. We feel the intensity of Imogen's devotion to Posthumus through the vividness of her words describing how she would have fixed her eyes on the disappearing figure of her husband till he had seemed as small as a needle, and had finally seemed to merge with the sky like a gnat melting into the air. And Posthumus's love for her is just as strongly communicated through the image of him standing on deck and waving his glove, hat, or handkerchief as if to make his gesture say that his ship might be sailing swiftly away, but his soul was leaving Imogen with the utmost slowness and reluctance. Likewise, the very things that Imogen was unable to say to Posthumus—that he should share certain thoughts and prayers with her at particular hours, and that he must take care not to be tempted by the girls of Italy, where he is going—these things become as real in the language as if they had actually happened. (And, of course, there is the further subtle hint that if they had 'happened', if they had been presented as one of the enacted scenes of the play, they would still not have taken place in the real world to which the audience belong. Whether acted out by Imogen and Posthumus, or only imagined by Imogen, as here, they would be equally part of a dramatic fiction.)

NOTES AND GLOSSARY:
Senseless: unable to feel
orisons: prayers

Act I Scene 4

Posthumus reaches Rome, where he is introduced to a company of gallants, among them Iachimo. A Frenchman refers to a previous occasion when he had met Posthumus and to a quarrel, which had come near to being a duel, over the honour of Posthumus's lady (Imogen). This prompts Iachimo to a number of cynical remarks about women's chastity, and he taunts Posthumus with the assertion that his lady cannot possibly be the perfectly virtuous woman that he claims.

Posthumus allows himself to be provoked by this, and lays a wager with Iachimo on Imogen's honour: Posthumus stakes the ring which Imogen gave him (in Act I Scene 1) against the 10,000 ducats waged by Iachimo that the latter will not be able to seduce her. If Iachimo wins there will be no further quarrel between them, but if he fails, he will have to fight a duel with Posthumus. They strike a bargain, and Iachimo declares that he will set off for Britain immediately.

This scene is essential to the plot; without the wager the Imogen–Posthumus–Iachimo story cannot go forward. But given the character attributed to Posthumus at the beginning of the play, and the importance which he attaches to his ring as a pledge of Imogen's love, it is difficult to believe that he would descend so low as to engage in a bet on her virtue. Shakespeare gets round the problem, however, by creating an atmosphere of fashionable cynicism. This is the world portrayed in the poem 'Go and catch a falling star' by the Elizabethan poet John Donne (1572–1637). In this, the person to whom the poem is addressed is told that even if he is lucky enough to find a woman who is both 'true *and* fair', he need not bother to write about it, for

> Though she were true when you met her,
> And last till you write your letter,
> Yet she
> Will be
> False, ere I come, to two or three.

Iachimo is the equivalent of the youthful John Donne, witty, quick in repartee, provocative, and affecting a mocking attitude of disillusionment with regard to women. For him there are no spiritual values; there are only appetite and materialism. Consequently a wager which attempts to put monetary value on virtue is quite appropriate to him, inappropriate though it may be to Posthumus. His language betrays the corruption that goes with such a view: 'If you buy ladies' flesh at a million a dram you cannot preserve it from tainting' (lines 129–31).

Posthumus, precisely because he finds this outlook so repulsive, falls a comparatively easy prey to such cynicism. He does not at once agree, of course; but when Iachimo interprets his reluctance as lack of confidence in Imogen, this stings him, as Iachimo had intended it should do, into accepting the wager. His action is thus made plausible without being excused. Indeed, the reaction of Philario, who tries to discourage the wager ('It came in too suddenly; let it die as it was born', lines 115–16), makes it clear that the whole thing is rash and ill-considered. The most that can be said for Posthumus is that his belief in Imogen is so strong that he is absolutely confident that she will stand the test. What he does not understand is the combination of cynicism and slickness which he is encountering for the first time in Iachimo.

NOTES AND GLOSSARY:

crescent note: increasing reputation

So your brace ... casual: so your pair of things which you regard as priceless, the one is subject to human frailty and the other to chance

convenience: overcome

moiety: half

a million a dram: a million ducats for a very small quantity

tainting: pollution, corruption

Act I Scene 5

In Britain again the Queen asks Cornelius, a physician, if he has brought certain drugs which she ordered. Cornelius produces them, but with reluctance, because, he says, they are poisons which cause a slow death. The Queen replies that she merely wants to test their properties. We learn, however, in an aside from Cornelius, that he does not trust her, and so has deceived her by giving her drugs which will only produce an appearance of death; after a time the being to whom they are given will revive, and be refreshed. Pisanio enters. The Queen tries to persuade him to wean Imogen's love from Posthumus, and make her love Cloten instead. She offers him promotion and rewards if he will do this, and slyly drops the box of poisons, intending that Pisanio will pick it up, as he does. It is a restorative medicine, she says, and she insists that Pisanio keep it, as a first favour to be followed by others. Her real purpose, however, is to induce Pisanio to take it, and so poison himself, by which means she hopes to get rid of a servant whom she believes to be too faithful to Posthumus.

Cornelius's attitude towards the Queen, and her own interest in 'confections' and poisons, confirms the impression of her as a witch-like character. She also has a natural antipathy towards goodness, as we see in her attitude towards Pisanio. To her he is 'a flattering rascal' (line 27)—which, of course, is the precise opposite of the truth. She makes some attempt to win him over to her side, but she does not expect to succeed. Thus it is that she offers him inducements to betray Posthumus; but even while she is doing this she contrives the dropping of the box, which, she hopes, will rid her of Pisanio for ever. She knows that he is a danger to her cause since he will be a constant reminder to Imogen of the pledge given to Posthumus (lines 77-8); but, she adds (with delight in the prospect), if Pisanio takes the poison himself, Imogen will then be deprived of any ambassadors from her sweet-heart (lines 78–80). The ingrained viciousness of the Queen is further indicated by her conclusion that Imogen will be made to taste the poison as well, if she does not change her mind. However, the final words of the scene reassure the audience that Pisanio is determined to remain faithful to Posthumus.

NOTES AND GLOSSARY:

confections: drugs

prove: test

Think what a chance thou changest on: think both of the risk and the opportunity you have if you switch sides

remembrancer: one who will remind her (Imogen)

to hold/The hand-fast: to keep her contract

unpeople her/Of leigers for her sweet: deprive her of ambassadors who will carry her messages to her sweetheart

Act I Scene 6

The scene opens with Imogen lamenting her isolated situation: her father unkind, her stepmother hypocritical, harrassed by Cloten's foolish suit, and separated from her banished husband. For a moment she wishes that she, too, like her brothers, had been stolen away when a child. Pisanio announces the arrival of Iachimo, who brings with him a letter of introduction from Posthumus. Iachimo's first reaction on seeing her is to despair of winning his bet, but he quickly collects his wits and begins his attempt. He pretends to be struck with amazement, speaking in puzzling terms of man's ability to make difficult distinctions and yet failure to distinguish obvious goodness from badness. He gets rid of Pisanio by sending him with a message for his servant, and then continues his plan by telling Imogen how merry Posthumus is in Rome. Then he begins to hint that Posthumus has been unfaithful to Imogen, while expressing extreme horror that he could be faithless to such a beautiful woman. He then becomes more direct in his accusations, saying that he pities Imogen, and urging her to take revenge. Imogen is puzzled by this, but it quickly emerges that Iachimo is offering her the opportunity to get her own back by making love with him. Imogen is immediately horrified and disgusted; she calls for Pisanio and threatens to report Iachimo to her father. Iachimo, realising that this particular strategy has failed, extricates himself by pretending that all he has suggested was simply a test of Imogen's constancy to Posthumus, and he offsets his calumny of Posthumus by now praising him to the skies. This mollifies Imogen; but Iachimo has merely changed his plan. Taking advantage of Imogen's restored trust he asks her to look after a trunk for him which, he says, contains, a valuable gift for the Roman Emperor. Imogen agrees, and offers her own bedroom as the best place for its safekeeping overnight. Iachimo says he must embark next morning, and offers to carry a letter from Imogen to Posthumus.

The isolation of Imogen at the beginning of the scene emphasises the vulnerable position in which she has been left. It thus heightens the tension when Iachimo begins his attempt on her. Pisanio is a link with Posthumus, but Iachimo's ruse to get rid of him ensures that Imogen will face her crisis in total isolation.

But if this is in the tragic mood of the play, the reference which she makes (lines 5–7) to her lost brothers, Guiderius and Arviragus, is another reminder (comparable to Act I Scene 1, lines 57–67) of characters who will eventually be part of a countervailing, anti-tragic movement. It is significant that 'happy' (line 6) is the word coupled with them. The succeeding sentence, 'but most miserable/ Is the desire that's glorious' (lines 6–7), is clearly meant as a contrast. Imogen is thinking of the difference between peril at court and happiness away from it. This is a common theme of pastoral literature (called 'pastoral' because it is nominally about shepherds and shepherdesses, but in essence it is a form of literature which contrasts the pure and simple country life with the corrupt sophistication of court and city life). Imogen's words anticipate what is to come later in the play; and that they do indeed have pastoral overtones seems to be confirmed by lines 7–9: blessed are those, no matter how lowly their status may be, who 'have their honest wills' (their 'plain' desires, but also 'honest' in the sense of 'virtuous', and with an implied contrast to the dishonest desires typical of the court), for this makes their comfort seem all the better.

Iachimo's reaction on first seeing Imogen is perhaps the highest tribute to her. Such is her beauty, and so closely linked is it with a sense of spiritual as well as bodily perfection, that even the extreme cynic, Iachimo, concedes for a moment that she might be incomparable, like the phoenix, and that therefore he has already lost his bet. However, he calls on audacity to strengthen his resolve.

In the event Iachimo's first attack is a frontal one, but nonetheless carried out with deviousness. He muses aloud in words that are calculated to puzzle Imogen, but also to start her thoughts running in the channels which suit Iachimo's purpose.

Are men insane? he wonders (lines 31–7). Has nature given them eyes to see heaven and earth, and to distinguish between the planets in the sky above and stones which look so much like one another and lie in such plentiful numbers on the beach; and yet (here he switches to first person plural) can 'we' not, with eyes of such rare nature, make distinction between beautiful and ugly?

Then he continues (lines 38–45): this fault cannot be in the eye, for apes and monkeys confronted with a 'fair' and a 'foul' woman would chatter their approval of Imogen and show by grimaces their condemnation of her opposite; nor in the reason, for even idiots in this particular case of beauty would have enough wisdom to make the right choice; nor in the desire, for the slut, when compared with such elegant perfection, ought to make desire retch with disgust (or vomit till the stomach is empty and has nothing left in it any longer) and lose its taste for such food.

Finally (lines 46–9), Iachimo, without quite stating that he is doing so, offers an explanation of the extreme case of perversity which he has been supposing: it is cloyed lust—that form of desire which when satisfied still remains unsatisfied, that tub which no matter how often it is filled still drains away—which bolts down the lamb, and then afterwards longs for garbage.

The meaning of these speeches becomes clearer both to Imogen and the audience as the scene proceeds. Iachimo is hinting that Posthumus has been unfaithful. But as yet he does not say so directly. When Imogen asks him if Posthumus is cheerful (line 57), he seizes the opportunity to suggest that Posthumus is extravagantly merry, as if he felt no distress at all at being parted from Imogen. Iachimo goes on to attribute to Posthumus the very cynicism with regard to women which Iachimo himself had expressed in Act I Scene 4. But this is completely out of character with the Posthumus known to Imogen, and so she remains sceptical. Iachimo, therefore, makes it a little clearer that the perversion of taste to which he had been obliquely referring earlier is, in fact, Posthumus's. What a deplorable thing it is, he says, to hide away from the bright sun and take comfort in a dungeon lit by the wick of a candle (lines 84–6). This at last disturbs Imogen, and she demands to know outright what he has to say about Posthumus. Still, however, Iachimo replies, not by saying that Posthumus does so and so, but by saying 'If *I* had such a cheek [gazing adoringly at Imogen's] to kiss, and abandoned it for a prostitute's, such treachery would deserve all the torments that hell could muster' (lines 98–111). He thus at once accuses Posthumus, and slyly insinuates himself into Posthumus's place as lover of Imogen. He then redoubles the revulsion which such treachery is likely to arouse by repeated references to the disgustingly diseased nature of the women with whom, he implies, Posthumus is keeping company. This, he hopes, will so arouse Imogen's anger that she will want to take revenge on Posthumus, and, having in effect asked why should Imogen be confined to cold chastity while Posthumus spends her money on prostitutes, he thereupon offers himself as both a form of revenge and a compensation for what Iachimo, being the sort of man he is, cannot help regarding as an abstinence that Imogen must resent.

When this strategy misfires, Iachimo shows his intelligence and resourcefulness by immediately switching to another plan. The audience, of course, does not know at this stage what it is. Indeed, to those seeing the play for the first time, and ignorant of the story on which it was based, it might well have seemed that Iachimo was admitting defeat and simply covering his retreat by rather fulsome praise of Posthumus.

But he seems, instead, to have chosen the 'Parthian' tactics of 'flying flight' (line 20). He is going to leave Britain the next day, and the request to leave the trunk with Imogen seems a perfectly innocent one. Imogen at least thinks so, and makes Iachimo's second plan easier for him by offering of her own accord to keep it in her room. It is possible that the plan was already devised by Iachimo before he left Rome as an alternative to the direct assault, since he obviously has a trunk of suitable size available; but, if so, no allusion is made to it, so that the effect is still that of an on-the-spur-of-the-moment inspiration. The audience is left surprised, but the biggest surprise—what happens in Act II Scene 2—is still to come.

NOTES AND GLOSSARY:

most miserable/Is the desire that's glorious: according to J. M. Nosworthy this means: 'most miserable is the unfulfilled longing that aspires to great things' (Arden edition, p.33); but Imogen, as her next words show, seems to be thinking of the miseries of court life contrasted with the quietness of humble country life

Blessed be those ... seasons comfort: blessed are those, no matter how lowly their status may be, who have their plain desires (but 'honest wills' also means 'virtuous desires'), for this makes their comfort taste the better

Arabian bird: the phoenix—a mythical bird, supposedly to be found in Arabia. There was only one of its kind; every 500 years it was said to burn itself to death and be reborn from its own ashes

Parthian: the Parthians, inhabitants of the region to the south-east of the Caspian Sea, fought on horseback and, when appearing to retreat, turned in the saddle to shoot arrows at the pursuing enemy

sadness: gravity, seriousness

tomboys: prostitutes

diseas'd ventures: prostitutes, infected with venereal disease, who offer themselves in the market-place

boil'd stuff: infected creatures who have received sweating treatment for their diseases

Diana's priest: Diana was the Roman goddess of chastity and hunting; her priest would have to abstain from sexual contact

affiance: faith (Iachimo claims to have been testing whether Imogen is true to Posthumus)

a holy witch:	a good, as opposed to a wicked, witch (not confined to the female sex only). Posthumus is so virtuous that he attracts people to him as if by magic
to fan:	separate the wheat from the chaff (test Imogen). But Imogen is so good she is 'chaffless' (line 177)
curious:	careful, anxious
short my word:	come short of my word
Gallia:	France

Act II Scene 1

Cloten complains about his failure to win at a game of bowls, and professes to regret that his rank prevents him from fighting with inferiors. One of the lords who attend him seems to agree with him, but expresses contempt for his foolishness in a series of asides. The scene concludes with a soliloquy from this same lord expressing his real admiration for Imogen and concern for the plight in which she is placed by her father's and stepmother's opposition to Posthumus.

Cloten's behaviour strengthens the impression already formed in the minds of the audience that he is an ignorant fool, quite unworthy of his rank, although he continually harps on the privileges this gives him. A number of puns (a favourite form of Shakespearean humour) play on this combination of worth and unworthiness.

The scene does not, however, make any very great contribution to the development of the play. It is mainly functional—acting as a time-filler between Act I Scene 6 and Act II Scene 2, and enabling the necessary preparations for the succeeding bedroom scene to be made.

NOTES AND GLOSSARY:

rank:	pun on the meanings of 'degree' and 'smell'
derogation ... derogate:	Cloten asks if it would lower his dignity to go and see Iachimo. The Second Lord replies that Cloten is so noble that there is no possibility of baseness in anything he does; but 'You cannot derogate' also means that Cloten cannot get any worse than he already is
cock ... capon ... comb:	word-play on 'fighting-cock', 'castrated cock' and 'fool' (*capon*), and a cock's 'comb', or crest, and 'coxcomb' (= fool, fop)

Act II Scene 2

Iachimo's trunk has been placed in Imogen's bedchamber, the location of this scene. When, tired from reading, she goes to sleep, Iachimo emerges from the trunk. He admires Imogen's beauty, and (to add circumstantial evidence to his tale when he returns to Rome) takes notes on the furnishing and decoration of her room. But since he thinks that some intimate personal details will be more convincing, he also notes certain marks on her body—in particular a five-spotted mole—and removes a bracelet from her arm. The clock strikes, and Iachimo returns to the trunk.

In contrast to the previous scene this one is intensely dramatic and poetically vivid. Imogen's opening question, 'Who's there?' reflects the audience's own apprehensiveness, and the fact that it is 'almost midnight' (line 2) activates their superstitious dread of midnight. Her statement that 'Sleep hath seiz'd me wholly' (line 7) helps to explain why in the subsequent part of the scene she is so oblivious of all that Iachimo is doing, but it also suggests that she is for the time being a helpless prisoner of unconsciousness. Again we have the theme of the isolated and vulnerable Imogen.

Iachimo's speech on emerging from the tunk is complex in its poetic effects. Not everything he says should be judged in terms of character. It is not the cynical Iachimo who gives such lyrically beautiful expression to the chastity and loveliness of the sleeping Imogen so much as Shakespeare, the poet, putting words into Iachimo's mouth which make the audience more intensely aware of the contrast between his wicked deceitfulness and her natural innocence. The reference to Tarquin, lines 12–14:

> Our Tarquin thus
> Did softly press the rushes ere he waken'd
> The chastity he wounded

does not of course mean that Iachimo is about to imitate Tarquin's act of rape, but it adds a sense of horror, and of threat to Imogen, which greatly increases the audience's fears for her. Morover, if Iachimo is not about to commit an act of violence on Imogen, he is about to do something which will destroy her reputation in Posthumus's eyes, thus committing what amounts to a moral rape.

In contrast to these associations of lust, violence and darkness, Imogen is associated with whiteness (line 16) and purity (symbolised by the lily, line 15). Her eyes are described as 'lights' hidden behind her window-like eyelids, to which the flame of her taper is so attracted that it 'bows toward her' (with the further suggestion of paying reverential respect to her), and it strives to peep under those eyelids to see the eyes beneath, as if light is attracted towards greater light (lines 19–22). The colour blue is also associated with her, and since this is the symbolic colour of the Virgin Mary it accords with the emphasis on white: it is a 'blue of heaven's own tinct' (line 23).

The superlative quality of Imogen is suggested by the image of her lips as 'Rubies unparagon'd' and the poetic idea that it is her breath which gives such a sweet scent to the room (lines 18–19); and her oneness with nature is conveyed, not only by the 'fresh lily' reference, but also by the beautiful description of the mole on her left breast:

A mole cinque-spotted, like the crimson drops
I' th' bottom of a cowslip.   (Lines 38–9)

This converts what might otherwise be thought of as a minor physical defect into something with a highly individual, but also completely natural beauty of its own.

Some of the details of the room which Iachimo notes down are not explained until Act II Scene 4, and this is done so as not to spoil their dramatic effect in the later scene. We do learn, however, that Imogen has been reading about the rape of Philomela. This takes us back to the rape theme. It tells the audience, in effect, that the outrage anticipated by the image of Tarquin moving over the rush-strewn floor (lines 12–13) has now been completed, and it is time for Iachimo to return to the trunk. Dawn is near (lines 48–9, and the chiming of the hours counted by Iachimo at line 51), but, with a brilliant summing up of the contrast on which the scene has been based, Iachimo's re-entry into the trunk is associated with hell (as if he were descending again into the dark, infernal region from which he had come) and Imogen's innocence makes her seem angelic: 'Though this a heavenly angel, hell is here' (line 50). Thus it concludes a scene which greatly affects the plot, but which Shakespeare also makes the occasion for a striking symbolic contrast between good and evil.

NOTES AND GLOSSARY:

midnight: a time of superstitious dread. Evil spirits were believed to walk about at midnight (the 'fairies' of line 9 are supernatural beings of a wicked kind) and tempt men to crimes, hence Imogen's prayer at lines 9–10

Tarquin: Sextus Tarquinius, the son of Tarquinius Superbus, last of the semi-legendary kings of Rome, supposedly raped Lucretia, the wife of Lucius Tarquinius Collatinus, who first told her husband what had happened and then committed suicide. Shakespeare tells the story in his poem, *The Rape of Lucrece* (1594), and in *Macbeth* (II.1.52–6) he evokes the scene when Tarquin crept through the night towards Lucretia's room with a similar sense of horror

bravely:	splendidly
Cytherea:	Venus, goddess of love
unparagon'd:	without equal

windows white and azure, lac'd: the Signet text (p.74) reads 'white and azure-laced', a preferable reading since it better suggests the effect of eyelids which are pure white, but streaked with the heaven-like blue of Imogen's veins

cinque-spotted: five-spotted; the five-part arrangement (or 'quincunx') had mystical significance in the seventeenth century

tale of Tereus ... Philomel: one of the stories of Greek mythology retold by the Latin poet, Ovid (BC43–18AD) in his *Metamorphoses* (Book IV), a work well known to Shakespeare. Philomela was raped by Tereus, the husband of her sister, Procne, and to prevent her telling what had happened Tereus cut out her tongue. But Philomela wove a tapestry which revealed the story to Procne, and the two sisters took revenge by killing Tereus's son, Itys, and causing the father to eat the son's flesh. At the end Philomela, Procne and Tereus were turned into birds. (See *The Metamorphoses of Ovid*, translated by Mary M. Innes, Penguin books, Harmondsworth, 1955, pp.159–66.)

Act II Scene 3

Morning has come, and Cloten orders musicians to serenade Imogen with the song, 'Hark, hark! the lark'. Cymbeline and the Queen enter and enquire about Cloten's success in wooing, the Queen advising him to show persistence. A messenger arrives to announce the approach of an embassy from Rome led by Caius Lucius. The King and Queen go to receive him, while Cloten stays behind to greet Imogen. When Imogen enters, however, she is as unwilling as ever to listen to Cloten's suit. He maintains that she is guilty of disobedience by not yielding to her father's wish that she should abandon Posthumus for himself; he then begins to abuse Posthumus. But this merely provokes Imogen to tell him how unworthy he is compared with Posthumus. She calls Pisanio, and asks him to search for her lost bracelet, about which she is very anxious.

Contrast is also emphasised in this scene, too, though here the contrast is between the oafishness and vulgarity of Cloten and the greater dignity, and loyalty to her husband, of Imogen. There is also a contrast between the music which Cloten uses as part of his wooing and the coarse puns which Cloten uses in talking about it. It is also characteristic of Cloten that he should try to bribe Imogen's lady-in-waiting, but there is no indication that he is successful in doing so.

The arguments used by Cloten in his attempt to persude Imogen that her marriage to Posthumus is not binding (lines 111–24) are slightly above his intellectual capacity. They are based on the ideas of order and obedience which were greatly respected by the Elizabethans, but Cloten uses them for selfish ends.

Cloten begins with Imogen's obedience to her father. This was a cardinal principle, which Imogen would not deny outright; but we have already seen that Cymbeline, under the evil influence of the Queen, is not being his truly rational, kingly self, and that Imogen has made a choice which all right-thinking people approve. Essentially, then, Imogen remains true to the requirements of order; her disobedience is apparent rather than real.

And then, if Cloten had any case at all, he straight away spoils it by attacking Imogen's 'contract' (marriage) to Posthumus on the grounds that marriage only binds common people who have no social position of any consequence. Being a princess, she does not have such freedom to choose for herself. This particular argument is one which would have had some force in Shakespeare's day, when royal marriages did, indeed, have great political significance; and the suggestion that Imogen has committed a serious offence by marrying beneath her own rank would likewise be taken seriously. But the true worth of Posthumus remains an essential part of Imogen's defence, and the fact that Cloten is the proposed alternative greatly undermines the argument drawn from nobility of rank. That Cloten finally descends to the level of personal abuse shows yet again how unworthy of his own position he is.

The main thing here, however, is that Shakespeare here clearly exalts marriage (especially that which, in his Sonnet 116, he calls 'the marriage of true minds') above political expediency. Such marriage is itself a symbol of the spiritual harmony (it knits souls — see line 117) to which the ideal of order is directed, and in keeping faith with her husband Imogen is showing that fundamental respect for order on which, in the Shakespearean view, the health of society and of mankind depends. What is at stake is not mere conformity to the powers-that-be, but a profound, inward sense of order.

Cloten drops back to his more customary level when he shows that what especially riles him in Imogen's reply is her assertion that the most trivial garment which ever touched Posthumus's body means more to her than all the hairs on Cloten's head, even if each one were made into such a man as he is (lines 133–6). The word 'garment' sticks in his throat, and it becomes his final exit line. This is dramatically effective as it points forward to the later use made of clothes to disguise appearances.

NOTES AND GLOSSARY:

penetrate:	have an emotional effect (but with a bawdy pun on the meaning, 'gain sexual entry')
horsehairs:	bow-strings
calves' guts:	fiddle-strings
unpaved eunuch:	castrato
Prefer:	advance, recommend
senseless:	the Queen uses the word to mean 'deaf' (she advises Cloten not to listen if Imogen tries to send him away), but Cloten stupidly takes it to mean that he is a fool
meaner:	of lower rank
A hilding for a livery:	a nobody fit only to wear servant's clothes
pantler:	servant in the pantry
clipp'd:	embraced

Act II Scene 4

In Rome once more Posthumus and Philario are talking about Posthumus's exile from Britain. They also discuss the quarrel which is developing over tribute which Britain refuses to pay to Rome. Caius Lucius is the Roman ambassador in this matter, and Philario expects him to be successful; but Posthumus patriotically maintains that the British are too brave to give in. Iachimo enters, delivers Imogen's letter to Posthumus, and insinuates that he has won the bet. As proof he offers, first, a description of Imogen's bedchamber and its ornaments, which Posthumus, however, rejects on the ground that Iachimo might simply have heard these details being spoken about. Then Iachimo follows this up by showing the bracelet, given to him, he claims, by Imogen herself. Posthumus is still unconvinced: the bracelet might have been intended for himself, he says. But when Iachimo asks if there are any words to that effect in the letter, Posthumus admits that there are not, and bitterly denounces Imogen. Philario tries to restrain him, suggesting that the bracelet may have been stolen, but when Iachimo produces his third piece of supposed evidence—the identification of a mole beneath Imogen's breast—Posthumus abandons all belief in her virtue. He storms off the scene, declaring that he will return to the British court and tear Imogen limb from limb in front of her father.

To the reader, this scene might well give the impression that Posthumus is too credulous. Iachimo's supposed evidence is circumstantial only, and it should be quite inadequate to undermine the conviction of a thoughtful and rational person. Indeed, the more detached Philario shows just that scepticism which might have been expected from Posthumus himself. But in the theatre, where things move rapidly without leisure for reflection, and where emotions have by this time been thoroughly aroused, it will seem more plausible that Posthumus should be deceived.

The scene is, moreover, a natural sequel to Act I Scene 4, where Posthumus, because of his very goodness, falls an easy prey to the sophisticated cynicism of Iachimo. The latter is very adroit in his handling of Posthumus. He starts with his weakest evidence first, which he knows can be refuted, but which serves its purpose nevertheless by suggesting a degree of intimacy between Imogen and Iachimo that is emotionally disturbing to Posthumus. The production of the bracelet— flashed under Posthumus's nose in a highly tantalising way, and then pocketed again—constitutes a much more serious challenge to Posthumus's confidence in Imogen. He parries with the rather shaky 'May be she pluck'd it off/To send it me' (lines 103–4), but in so doing gives Iachimo the opportunity for a very neat rejoinder: 'She writes so to you, doth she?' (line 104). Iachimo can thus make the absence of any reference to the bracelet in Imogen's letter (written, of course, before the theft had even taken place) seem an incriminating omission. The damage it does is revealed in Posthumus's contemptuous reference to the ring, hitherto the symbol of Imogen's faith to him, as a 'basilisk' (line 107), and his extravagant wish that honour and beauty should be divorced, and that women's vows should have no binding effect on those to whom they are made since women themselves have no real virtue (lines 108–112).

Philario's greater caution makes Posthumus relent for a moment, but he is easily convinced now by Iachimo's oath, 'By Jupiter' (line 121); and the final, triumphant reference to the mole (coupled with what purports to be a sensual reminiscence of kissing it) completes Iachimo's deception of the embittered Posthumus.

Such apparent disillusionment has almost tragic dimensions. At the same time, however, it is tinged with the absurd. Posthumus is no longer himself. Although 'By Jupiter' had been so convincing to him before, when Iachimo again undertakes to swear he exclaims, in words that can only strike the audience as highly ironic,

> No swearing.
> If you will swear you have not done't, you lie;
> And I will kill thee if thou dost deny
> Thou'st made me cuckold.
>
> (lines 143–6)

Posthumus has been brought to the point where he will not believe the truth, but only its opposite. By putting it as baldly as this, however, he appears in a somewhat ridiculous light. We pity him that his virtue makes him so vulnerable to Iachimo (and we are very anxious for

Imogen), but we are also a little inclined to laugh at a man who expresses such an extravagant attitude. This is confirmed by his exit line. He utters the terrible threat to tear Imogen 'limb-meal' (line 147), but goes out on the unfinished sentence, 'I'll do something—' (line 149), with an effect of bathos. As Philario says, he is 'Quite besides/The government of patience!' (lines 149–50), but somewhere at the bottom of our minds we feel that he must eventually come to his senses again.

NOTES AND GLOSSARY:

knowledge of: both 'information about' and 'sexual experience with'

the story, / Proud Cleopatra ... the banks: refers to the occasion when Cleopatra, Queen of Egypt, first met the great Roman general, Mark Antony, on the River Cydnus. It is the subject of one of the most famous speeches in Shakespeare's *Antony and Cleopatra* (II.2.189–222)

Chaste Dian bathing: the picture of Diana is appropriate to Imogen because she is as chaste as the goddess; but there is a hint, too, that it concerns Actaeon, who was punished by being torn to death by his own hunting dogs because he saw the goddess bathing—an outrage with which Iachimo's spying on Imogen may be compared

winking Cupids: 'winking' = blind; Cupid is the son of Venus, himself a god of love, represented as blind to show that love makes no rational choice

basilisk: mythical creature whose eyes could kill

By Jupiter: an oath sworn by the greatest of the gods (Roman version of Greek Zeus), which makes Iachimo's falsehood the more shocking, but also makes Posthumus's credulity more plausible. It is significant that the god who appears in Act V Scene 4, line 93, 'in thunder and lightening, sitting upon an eagle', is also Jupiter

stain: a serious pun on 'stain' meaning 'slight physical blemish', and 'stain' meaning 'moral pollution'

Act II Scene 5

Posthumus soliloquises on the viciousness of women.

Though printed in modern editions as a separate scene, this is in effect a continuation of the previous scene. It shows the irrationality and absurdity of Posthumus, in what he takes to be his disillusionment with

Imogen, carried to the extreme. His revulsion is so strong that he condemns not only his wife, but his mother and the female sex in general. Is it not possible for men to come into the world, he asks, without women being involved? Because he now believes Imogen to be false he thinks that all women must be so, and therefore every birth illegitimate. He can still remember clearly enough that his mother and Imogen were reckoned as paragons of chastity, but his disgust is so extravagant that he now thinks of them in terms appropriate to whores. Iachimo is imagined as a boar mounting a sow—words are unnecessary, a grunt of lust is enough to get him what he wants. Even more preposterous is the suggestion that any vices that men may have derive solely from those elements which they take from their mothers (lines 20–2). He will denounce women in satirical writings, he says; but he decides finally that it is better to let them have what they want, for their desires are so evil that by having them fulfilled they will be as damned as the devil could wish (lines 32–4).

Posthumus's language in this speech is as gross and sordid as that of Iachimo himself—if not worse. Iachimo has thus succeeded in imposing on Posthumus his own coarse vision of a world which only professes virtue and is in reality sexually depraved. At the same time the ideas which Posthumus expresses are so absurd, and the words he uses are so extravagant, that the audience is left in no doubt of the complete falsity and unreasonableness of such a view.

NOTES AND GLOSSARY:

prudency: modesty
Saturn: father of the gods, associated with cold and melancholy
Nice: here means 'lascivious'

Act III Scene 1

Caius Lucius arrives at Cymbeline's court to demand renewal of the tribute which Julius Caesar had exacted from Britain during the reign of Cassibelan. He is refused. The Queen urges Cymbeline to remember that Britain is defended by a natural wall of water, and that he is descended from a line of brave kings. Cassibelan, indeed, came very near to defeating Caesar. Cloten joins in with defiance of the Romans, and Cymbeline insists that, Britain being a free nation, the tribute is unjust. Lucius then reluctantly declares war on behalf of Augustus Caesar against Britain. The scene ends with the offer of a courteous welcome to Lucius personally, but with continuing defiance of the power of Rome.

In this scene the evil character of the Queen and the stupidity of Cloten are overlaid by the patriotic emotions aroused by their speeches on Britain. It is perhaps typical that the Queen rather than Cymbeline is the first to defy the Romans, and in the light of subsequent events this may seem politically unwise; but the tone and substance of her speech in lines 14–33 are both meant to command the audience's support. Even Cloten's crude defiance of the Romans stirs a sympathetic response, for it is the national cause and independence of Britain which are at stake. The Queen's image of Britain as 'Neptune's park', fenced with unassailable rocks and surrounded with high seas and sinking sands, recalls John of Gaunt's speech in Shakespeare's *Richard II* (II.1.31–66) which represents England as

> This precious stone set in the silver sea,
> Which serves it in the office of a wall,
> Or as a moat defensive to a house,

and it is infused with a similarly patriotic fervour. In memorable words she makes the sea itself seem to have been a fighter against Julius Caesar, tossing his ships as if they were mere play-things and wrecking them on the rocks as easily as if they were egg-shells (lines 27–9). By this means she puts spirit into her husband, Cymbeline, so that he too has the courage to assert the freedom of Britain and to speak of her ancient laws which, he says, he is determined to restore to his people.

All of this would undoubtedly have gone down very well with Shakespeare's original audience; but it should also be noticed that Cymbeline is more respectful than the Queen or Cloten, not only to Lucius, but also to the idea of Rome as embodied in the person of the Emperor Augustus Caesar. He received his knighthood from Caesar and 'gather'd honour' (line 69) from him, and although he says that this very honour compels him to fight to the death if Caesar tries to take it back again, the impression is left that Cymbeline's true honour, and that of Britain, is tied to recognition of the dignity and authority of Rome.

NOTES AND GLOSSARY:

Augustus Caesar: Gaius Octavius (BC63–14AD) received the name 'Augustus' in BC27 when he became the first Roman emperor, and it was a title then given to later emperors

Julius Caesar: Gaius Julius Caesar (102–44BC), the most famous of all the Romans. He conquered France in his campaign of 59–51BC and landed in, but did not occupy, Britain. It is to this that the Queen refers when she says, 'A kind of conquest / Caesar made here' (lines 22–3); but when she adds that he 'made not here his brag / Of "came, and saw, and over-came"' she is translating the well-known words, *'veni, vidi, vici'*, in which Caesar announced his victory at Zela (47BC) in Asia Minor. He was stabbed to death in the Senate at Rome (15 March, 44BC), and this is the subject of Shakespeare's tragedy *Julius Caesar*

giglot: wanton

Lud's Town: London

crook'd noses: a hooked nose is known as a 'Roman nose'

Pannonians and Dalmatians: Pannonia is modern Hungary; Dalmatia is modern Yugoslavia

---

Act III Scene 2

Pisanio receives a letter from Posthumus apparently ordering him to murder Imogen for her supposed unfaithfulness, and implying that the letter which he has also sent to Imogen herself will cause her to provide Pisanio with an opportunity to do the deed. Pisanio, however, cannot believe that Imogen is guilty, and feels that it is Posthumus who has fallen into evil. Imogen enters and eagerly reads the letter which is given to her. In it Posthumus says that he has landed at Milford Haven and is impatient to see her. Imogen, fired with longing to see her husband again, demands to know how quickly she can get to Milford, and plans to make her departure immediately.

Pisanio's reaction to Posthumus's letter provides a welcome relief from Posthumus's own inversion of moral values in Act II Scene 5. He has no doubts about Imogen's innocence, and recognises that the 'service' which Posthumus demands of him would be a disservice. He wonders how he could seem to be lacking in humanity to such an extent as to be thought capable of committing a crime of this nature (lines 15–17)—which is a way of saying both that the murder of Imogen would be an act of the utmost inhumanity and that the humane Pisanio is appalled.

Imogen herself shows by the tenderness which she displays in opening the letter how deeply Posthumus is misjudging her; and her reaction to its contents—heightened by the broken-up syntax which suggests her breathless excitement—reveals her passionate enthusiasm for the prospect of reunion with her husband. In sharp contrast to the deviousness which Iachimo has displayed in his deception of Posthumus, and which this letter now suggests that Posthumus has, so to speak, learnt from him, Imogen is all spontaneous directness. Her husband has called her, and her every instinct is to answer him:

> There's no more to say;
> Accessible is none but Milford way.   (lines 80–1)

The scene thus ends directing the audience's attention to Wales.

NOTES AND GLOSSARY:

fact:	deed, crime
fedary:	accomplice
characters:	writing, letters
tables:	tablets in which notes are made
Cambria:	Wales
I see before me ... look through:	I see what is in front of me. What is on this side or that, and what will follow, are hidden by a fog which I cannot see through

---

Act III Scene 3

For the first time Cymbeline's lost sons, Guiderius and Arviragus, and their abductor, Belarius, appear on the stage. They inhabit a cave in the Welsh mountains, and it is as if emerging from this cave that they make their entrance. They address the heavens, and Belarius orders the boys to go hunting on the higher slopes of the mountains while he keeps to the flatter land. He praises the natural life, but the boys regret their lack of experience of the world. Belarius explains how he was driven from Cymbeline's court as the result of a false accusation that he was in league with the Romans. As the boys go off to their hunting, he admits, in a soliloquy, that the boys show their royal descent by their dissatisfaction with the limitations of the country life. He explains how he stole them from the court when they were little more than babies, as an act of revenge for the injustice that was done to himself. Ever since they have believed that Euriphile, their nurse, now dead, was their mother, and that Belarius is their natural father.

This scene introduces Guiderius and Arviragus and explains how it comes about that they are still alive, yet living in the Welsh mountains ignorant of their royal descent. To that extent it is a necessary furthering of the plot. But its main significance is thematic, and dependent on the pastoral convention which exalts the life of nature above the artificiality and duplicity of the court (see the more extended discussion of this subject in Part 3 of these Notes). In his somewhat didactic speeches Belarius gives a moral meaning to the life which he and the boys lead in their Welsh cave. The very fact that they have to stoop to pass through its entrance teaches them to bend down with proper humility and worship the heavens (the gods) in contrast with 'the gates of monarchs' which are so high that men are encouraged to be impiously proud and forget their religious duty (lines 1–7). When the boys are up on the mountains he will appear to them as no bigger than a crow, and this should teach them that it is only social position, not innate worth, which makes men seem inferior (lines 11–13). They should then go on to reflect that in courts opinion counts for more than service actually done (lines

14–17), and that the commoner is less exposed to danger than the mighty courtier. The latter lives in constant fear of rebuke, is bribed to do worthless things, and struts about in gorgeous clothes which merely run him into heavy debts, while none of these things affects the country-dweller (lines 21–6). The city is a place where money is lent out at extortionate rates of interest (lines 45–6), and the court inherently unstable, where one reaches high office only to lose it—or, which is just as bad, to be in perpetual fear of losing it (lines 46–9). The honour which soldiers seek at great personal risk is often enough taken away from them by slander, as, says Belarius, his own loss of Cymbeline's favour, through no fault of his own, goes to show (lines 49–70). All these are commonplaces of the pastoral tradition; as is Belarius's conclusion that he has enjoyed more 'honest freedom' and been more truly religious since he took to living in the mountains than in all the time he spent at court (lines 71–3).

To moralise in this way is not, however, to carry complete conviction. It may be appropriate to an older man, says Guiderius. Belarius can speak from actual experience, and what he says may well be true, but how can a younger man judge, if he has seen nothing else but the country life? And another view of the natural life is expressed by Arviragus which makes it seem very different from the 'honest freedom' which Belarius finds in it; for him it is a way of life which reduces him and his brother to the level of beasts—they have freedom, but only the freedom to enjoy their ignorance (lines 39–44).

That we are meant to sympathise with this protest against the limitations of the pastoral life is evident, not only in the vigour of the language given to Guiderius and Arviragus, but in the soliloquy uttered by Belarius after they have made their exit (lines 79–107). This, too, is a natural reaction ('How hard it is to hide the sparks of nature'), of which Belarius secretly approves. It shows that Guiderius and Arviragus have the true principle of royalty within them, and that this will make itself felt even though the facts of their birth are hidden from the boys. This is shown, too, by the way they react when Belarius narrates his own past deeds as a soldier: they instinctively want to do the same. And Belarius, being a true soldier, cannot help but admire them for feeling as they do. Their princely blood is such a powerful natural force within them that it shows in their behaviour; and though what Belarius has been saying about the superiority of the natural to the courtly life is supported by the evidence of his own career (and, of course, by what we have seen in some of the courtly scenes already enacted for us in this play, especially those relating to Cloten), the longing of Guiderius and Arviragus to see more of the world, and to put their youthful strength to nobler use than the mere hunting of wild animals is presented as wholly natural and praiseworthy. Nature is better than the court, but nature also prompts those of 'princely blood' to seek the wider arena afforded by the court for the display of their inherent virtues. Guiderius and Arviragus have something in them which demands greater scope than the Welsh mountains, and therefore we have a sense that this pastoral retreat, though healthy and vigorous, is insufficient.

NOTES AND GLOSSARY:

jet: swagger, strut
allow'd: given due recognition
The sharded beetle ... eagle: the wing-case of a beetle offers more protection than the wings of an eagle
keeps his books uncross'd: does not pay off his debts
A cell of ignorance ... a limit: a narrow room in which we are barred from knowledge of the world at large, like someone lying in bed and making journeys only in his imagination, like an area which an imprisoned debtor is forbidden to go beyond

---

Act III Scene 4

Imogen and Pisanio are on the road to Milford Haven. Imogen is eager for the meeting with Posthumus, but Pisanio has to show her the letter which he has received ordering him to kill her. She is appalled, and puts it down to his infatuation with some woman he has met in Rome. His betrayal will be enough, she says, to make all men be mistrusted. Nevertheless, she tells Pisanio to carry out his master's command, which Pisanio refuses to do. Instead, he suggests that she dress herself up as a boy and offer her services to Caius Lucius, who is due to arrive in Milford the next day. He must return to the court, lest her absence be blamed on him, but before going he gives her the box which he had received from the Queen (Act I Scene 5), thinking that if she is ill it will do her good.

In this scene it is Imogen's turn to believe that her lover is false, just as Posthumus had believed her to be false in Act II Scene 4. But, though she suspects him of having fallen in love with 'Some jay of Italy, / Whose mother was her painting', and in her distress regards Posthumus's example as one which will cause all virtuous men to be suspected of villainy, she does not fall into the mood of cynical disillusionment which possessed Posthumus. Hers is a condition of pathos rather than disgust; and even though she knows herself to be falsely accused she urges Pisanio to carry out his master's command. The sentence, 'The lamb entreats the butcher' (line 95), is indicative of the emotional quality of the scene: meekness and innocence in contrast with the persecutor. For Imogen the most painful thing is the change that has taken place in

Posthumus, and the fact that he is capable of calling her a 'strumpet'. It
does not, however, alter her own conception of her place *vis à vis*
Posthumus. Her sense of duty to him remains paramount.

All this, of course, makes Pisanio's situation also a tormented one. His
own loyalties are subjected to painful conflict. He is even ordered by
Imogen to show his loyalty to Posthumus by killing her, though he feels
that to do so would lead to damnation (lines 71–2). But he also shows
resourcefulness. He has already provided the clothes necessary for
Imogen's disguise, and he is practical in the advice he gives her on how to
imitate a boy. By this means he turns the situation from one which is
primarily distressful to one that is at least reasonably hopeful; and the
device by which he does this is a tried one of Shakespearean comedy—
the disguising of a girl as a boy, when that 'girl' is being played in the
theatre by a boy-actor! (Compare Rosalind as Ganymede in Shakespeare's *As You Like It*, and Viola as Cesario in Shakespeare's *Twelfth
Night*.)

The references to Lucius are also encouraging (Shakespeare seizes the
opportunity to further the favourable impression created by the Roman
ambassador, even though the Romans are now about to fight the
Britons), and by the end of the scene Imogen has so warmed to the
proposal that she can say enthusiastically that she has the courage of a
soldier for the attempt, and that she will undertake it with the courage of
a prince (lines 181–3)—which it is perhaps not too fanciful to see as
linking her with the spirit shown by her princely brothers in the previous
scene.

However, what once more darkens the end of the scene a little is
Pisanio's gift of the box given to him by the Queen. It is not the
comforting medicine which he takes it for. The Queen intended it to be
lethal. But that, too, has its brighter side, for the audience remembers
that Cornelius had substituted a less dangerous potion for the one the
Queen demanded. Thus the plot has dark elements, but they are
counterbalanced by lighter ones. The closing words of the scene are
hopeful.

NOTES AND GLOSSARY:

worms: snakes

Some jay of Italy,/Whose mother was her painting: an Italian whore who
depends on cosmetics for her appearance of beauty

false Aeneas: a Trojan who escaped from Troy after its sack by
the Greeks and made his way to Italy, where he was
supposed to have founded the Roman race. This
story is told in Vergil's *Aeneid* (30–19BC). On his
journey he falls in love with Dido, Queen of
Carthage, but deserts her—hence Imogen's 'false'

Sinon:	it was Sinon who persuaded the Trojans to bring the wooden horse within the walls of Troy. Unknown to them, Greek soldiers were hidden inside it, and this led to the fall of Troy. Sinon thus became a byword for treachery
tent:	probe
Titan:	Hyperion, god of the sun
Juno:	Roman equivalent of Greek Hera, Queen of the gods

Act III Scene 5

The scene opens with Cymbeline giving a ceremonial farewell to Lucius, as diplomatic custom requires, although war has now been declared between Britain and Rome. He then enquires about Imogen, who has not put in her daily appearance. The Queen hypocritically defends her, and says that her absence is due to illness, which Imogen had asked the Queen to tell Cymbeline, but which the Queen, owing to the pressure of state affairs, had forgotten to do. Cymbeline is afraid of something worse having happened, and goes to find out. Left alone, the Queen reveals her true feelings: she hopes that Pisanio has killed himself with the drug she gave him, and she wonders whether Imogen has given way to despair, or fled to join Posthumus. Either way, she says, suits her plans, since Imogen will thus have consigned herself to death or dishonour, and the Queen will presumably be able to secure the crown for Cloten. The latter, whom the Queen had sent after the King, re-appears with the news that Imogen has fled and that the King is in a rage. This also suits the Queen, as she hopes that it may lead to the death of the King. Cloten encounters Pisanio, whom he suspects of being involved in some intrigue with Imogen. He threatens Pisanio and demands information. In response Pisanio produces a letter (later in the play revealed to be a false one, devised by Pisanio for the occasion) which seems to consist of a message from Posthumus to Imogen asking her to meet him at Milford Haven. This prompts Cloten to hatch a scheme for disguising himself as Posthumus and pursuing Imogen to Milford Haven, where he intends to kill Posthumus, rape Imogen, and then drive her with blows back to the court. He orders Pisanio to procure a suit of Posthumus's clothes for him, which Pisanio does in a pretence of serving him, although he makes it clear, in comments to the audience, that he has no intention of betraying either Posthumus or Imogen, and that he will write secretly to Posthumus that Imogen is dead. He tells Cloten that Imogen can hardly have reached Milford yet, but he secretly hopes that she will have made her escape by now, and that Cloten's journey will be for nothing.

The plot is thickening, and the attention of the audience is held by the various possibilities which the action holds in store. What will be the outcome of the war that is now imminent? How dangerous is the Queen? Will she succeed in removing Imogen and even, it seems, Cymbeline himself from the British throne? Will Cloten manage to carry out his typically depraved scheme? (He is misled about Posthumus, who at this stage is still in Italy, but the audience is anxious lest he might reach Imogen before she can carry out her plan to become Lucius's servant.) How is Pisanio going to cope with his difficult situation, pretending to serve Cloten, but remaining true to Posthumus, and yet needing, for Imogen's sake, to deceive Posthumus, at least to the extent of making him believe that Imogen is dead?

And yet, as in previous scenes, tragic possibilities are laced with touches of the comic, or even the grotesque. In this scene it is the grotesque which is to the fore, manifested in Cloten's determination to carry out his plan dressed in Posthumus's clothes, since Imogen's declaration 'that she held the very garment of Posthumus in more respect' than his 'noble and natural person' (lines 137–9) still rankles with him (compare Act II Scene 3). Not only is Cloten coarse and brutal, but so foolish that he allows trivialities to dominate his purpose. For that reason he excites the audience's ridicule as much as their anxiety.

NOTES AND GLOSSARY:

thou that stand'st so for Posthumus: you who stand up for Posthumus so much (the Queen wants to be rid of Pisanio because he is, from her point of view, too loyal to Posthumus)

Satisfy me home: give me a thorough and convincing account

be a voluntary mute: say nothing

Labour be his meed: let the effort be its own reward (may Cloten get nothing for his trouble)

Act III Scene 6

The scene is set in Wales, before the cave of Belarius: Imogen enters 'in boy's clothes' (though the Folio text merely reads: 'Enter Imogen alone'). She is weary and hungry and has lost her way. Seeing the cave, she resolves to enter it, whether it contains friend or foe. Belarius, Guiderius and Arviragus enter, having finished the hunting referred to in Act III Scene 3. 'Polydore' (the assumed name given to Guiderius) has proved the best hunter, and so, in accordance with their agreement, Belarius and 'Cadwal' (Arviragus) will prepare the food and wait on him. They are so hungry, however, that they decide to eat some of the cold meat which they have in the cave, while the fresh meat is being cooked. This leads to Belarius's discovery of Imogen, who is inside the cave, and so ravenous that she has started to eat some of their food. She is frightened, but protests that she intended to pay for what she has taken. She gives her name as 'Fidele'. Belarius reassures her, offers her comfort, and tells Guiderius and Arviragus, who are immediately attracted by her charm, to bid her welcome. They all go into the cave together.

The Folio text begins a new scene ('Scena Septima', Scene 7) after the exit of Imogen at line 27, but most modern editors treat the entrance of Belarius, Guiderius and Arviragus as the continuation of Scene 6. Clearly, after making her initial speech Imogen goes into the inner-stage (which serves as the cave—see Part I, p.13) to see what she will find there, and at that point (without having seen her) the old man and the two youngsters come on to the main stage. When Guiderius makes his reference to the 'cold meat i' th' cave' (line 38), Belarius goes to look for it, and, at line 39, discovers Imogen already eating their 'victuals' (food). Presumably he does not go right into the cave, for the stage-direction at line 44 reads 'Re-enter Imogen' (the Folio text reads 'Enter Imogen'), implying that Imogen comes out to him. Finally, with Belarius's 'Fair youth, come in' (line 89) and the repeated 'Pray draw near' (first from Guiderius, line 92, then from Arviragus, line 94), Imogen accompanies the three male characters into the cave.

Pastoral themes are again apparent in this scene. In her opening speech Imogen moralises in similar fashion to Belarius in Act III Scene 3, maintaining, for example, that lying on the part of the rich is worse than when it is done by the poor for the sake of need (lines 12–13), and that prosperity and ease tend to make men cowards, whereas hardship cultivates toughness (lines 21–2). Belarius himself continues his moralising fashion in such remarks as those in lines 32–5: our appetites will make plain food seem tasty, and weariness can make one sleep soundly even on sharp, stony ground, whereas sluggish idleness makes even a feather-pillow seem hard. At this point Imogen and Belarius are, of course, unaware of each other's presence, but the similar colouring of their language makes it seem as if there is an increasingly natural affinity between them.

This is still more evident after Imogen has met him, and more particularly her unknown brothers, Guiderius and Arviragus. The pastoral note is very strong when Imogen offers gold: it is vigorously rejected by Arviragus (lines 53–5), money being regarded as a debasement of the natural life; and Imogen herself is so impressed by the natural dignity which she finds in the cave that she intensifies her pastoral moralising to the point of saying that if great men had a court no bigger than this cave, if they waited on themselves, and lived according to the dictates of their consciences, they could not (putting aside the flattery they receive from the fickle crowd) excel Guiderius and Arviragus. For their part, Guiderius and Arviragus also find in Imogen a natural affinity which is so powerful that Guiderius immediately feels that if she were a woman (!) he would wish to marry her (lines 68–70), and Arviragus decides to love her as a brother (line 71). Thus, their innate virtues draw them instinctively together, and to crown it all Imogen can wish—with a touching dramatic irony, since the audience know that what she wishes is the actual truth—that they were indeed her brothers. Then, she adds in an aside, her father's objection to her marriage to Posthumus would also be less strong, since she would no longer be the heir to the throne, and so nearer to being Posthumus's equal (lines 75–8).

NOTES AND GLOSSARY:
stomachs: appetites
resty: idle
Fidele: Imogen adopts a name which has some reference to her condition—'the faithful one'

Act III Scene 7

In Rome two senators inform the tribunes that the Emperor has commanded them to raise a force among the gentry to fight against Britain, since the ordinary soldiers are fully engaged in war against rebels elsewhere. These auxiliaries are to help the weakened legions under the command of Lucius.

This scene shows war coming nearer to Britain, and provides the explanation for Posthumus's subsequent appearance (Act V Scene 1) as a gentleman among the Roman forces.

Act IV Scene 1

Cloten, dressed in Posthumus's clothes, is on his way to what he believes to be the meeting-place of Imogen and Posthumus.

The grossness of Cloten's mind is again illustrated by the sexual innuendoes in which he indulges.

NOTES AND GLOSSARY:
a woman's fitness comes by fits: a woman's sexual appetite comes at odd times
imperceiverant: incapable of making proper distinctions
enforced: raped

Act IV Scene 2

Imogen is not well, and therefore Belarius suggests that she should stay
in the cave while he and Guiderius and Arviragus are out hunting.
Guiderius offers to stay behind with her; he feels a love for her as great as
that which he feels for his 'father', Belarius. Arviragus loves her even
more. Imogen, however, persuades them to go hunting, though she is
greatly moved by the naturalness of their affection. As medicine for her
sickness she takes some of the potion given her by Pisanio, and then goes
into the cave. The men are about to move off when Cloten enters. His
reference to 'runagates' (runaways), meant with regard to Posthumus
and Imogen, is understood by Belarius as referring to himself and
Guiderius and Arviragus. They being outlaws, he thinks an attempt is
being made to capture them. Guiderius decides to deal with Cloten,
while Belarius and Arviragus see if others are pursuing. Cloten tries to
arrest Guiderius, who spurns him, and they go out fighting. Belarius and
Arviragus return, and soon Guiderius re-enters, carrying Cloten's head.
Belarius fears that the killing of Cloten will cause a punitive expedition
to be sent out from the Court, but Guiderius feels neither guilty nor
afraid. He goes out to throw Cloten's head into a nearby stream.
Belarius tells Arviragus to help Imogen ('Fidele') to prepare their meal,
and then soliloquises on the natural royalty of the two young men.
Guiderius returns, and 'solemn music' is heard. It proves to be a funeral
anthem, played by Arviragus for the death (as it appears) of Imogen. He
enters with her in his arms, a lamentation follows, and Guiderius and
Arviragus speak the song 'Fear no more the heat o' th' sun', over her
body. Belarius, maintaining that respect must be paid to Cloten, because
he was the Queen's son, fetches Cloten's body, and the two (Imogen and
Cloten) are laid side by side, strewn with flowers. Imogen is left alone
with the headless body of Cloten, dressed (as it has been throughout this
scene) in the clothes of Posthumus. She wakes from what has been no
more than a deeply drugged sleep, and, on seeing Cloten's body, takes it
for that of Posthumus. She curses Pisanio, as it seems to her that he has
been in league with Cloten to bring about the death of Posthumus, and
that the effect of the drug which Pisanio gave her is evidence of his guilt.
She falls in a faint on the body of Cloten, still mistaking it for
Posthumus. At this point Lucius enters, at the head of the Roman forces
which have been sent against Cymbeline. A soothsayer accompanying
him prophesies victory, for he has had a dream of a Roman eagle
vanishing into the sun. Lucius discovers the headless corpse, with
Imogen lying upon it. Imogen recovers, declares that she is a page, and
that her master has been slain by mountain brigands. Lucius is touched,
and accepts her as his own page. First, however, Imogen asks that the

body of her 'master' should be buried. They all go out, intending to do this.

This scene (or series of scenes run together by the Elizabethan practice of continuous action) is crowded with varied and changing action which seems incredible and even at times absurd. Coincidence is pressed rather hard: not only has Imogen by chance found her way to the cave where her unknown brothers live, but chance brings Cloten there, dressed in her husband's clothes; and Cloten's death at the hands of Guiderius coincides with Imogen's taking of the potion which produces the semblance of death in her. For no apparent reason (though it is clearly necessary for the plot) Guiderius also cuts off Cloten's head, thus making possible Imogen's misidentification of the body. Coincidence then brings Lucius and the Romans to this very same spot, allowing Imogen to come under his protection. In addition to all this, actual death (Cloten's) and mere appearance of death (Imogen's) occur at the same time, and the noble and ignoble, the mean and the mighty, are confusingly mingled.

Shakespeare, however, knows what he is doing. His concentration of so many incredible events into one scene has a purpose. On awaking from her drugged sleep, Imogen (in a few brilliant lines of dramatic writing by Shakespeare—lines 292–308) at first thinks she is back where she was at the beginning of Act III Scene 6, when she had first set out for Milford Haven. Two beggars had told her that she could not miss the way (Act III Scene 6; lines 8–9) and now she seems to have been dreaming of her dialogue with them (Act IV Scene 2, lines 292–4). She finds herself lying beside a corpse! Reality seems like a dream; or it is so horrible that she hopes she is dreaming (line 298). She recalls what seems to have been her brief life as a cook to Belarius, Guiderius and Arviragus, but it seems to her that that must have been unreal—like a non-existent arrow, created out of vapours ascending to the brain, shot at nothing (lines 301–2). She struggles to sort dream from reality, but finds it impossible to do so: the dream persists. Even though she is awake, the dream seems to be outside her, as well as within her mind; not merely imagination, but something that is actually being experienced (lines 307–8). All this is a remarkable re-creation of the confused state of mind of someone recovering from unconsciousness induced by a drug; and it goes far towards giving some air of plausibility to the most absurd incident in the scene—Imogen's mistaking of Cloten for Posthumus. (This, however, is exaggerated in effect by the confidence with which she identifies the various parts of his body as godlike, and tragedy is turned into something more like comedy when she looks for 'his jovial face', only to find that it is missing.) But what this confusion between dream and reality does is to break down the distinction between the world as lived in and the world as imagined, and in so doing to stifle the audience's criticism of the incredibility and absurdity of what they are seeing enacted on the stage before their eyes. The very sympathy which they feel for Imogen's difficulty in distinguishing between dream and reality teaches them to accept a mingling of the two, and to tolerate the transference of coincidence and absurdity from the dream-world— where it seems appropriate—to the real world—where it seems preposterous. In any case, the 'real world' of *Cymbeline*, a play, is only make-believe—a poet's dream made to look real.

NOTES AND GLOSSARY:

citizen:	city-bred (and therefore debased)
precious varlet:	foolish rascal
mere:	utter, complete
snatches:	stammering
Hercules:	(the Greek Heracles), a legendary hero of exceptional strength
I am perfect:	I know full well
Civility:	civilisation, cultivated behaviour
That angel of the world:	that divine quality at work in earthly circumstances
Thersites:	the nastiest and most scurrilous of the Greeks who took part in the Trojan War
Ajax:	one of the Greek leaders in the Trojan War, second only to Achilles in his strength and bravery
bolt:	arrow
Mercurial:	like that of Mercury (the Greek Hermes), messenger of the gods, who wore winged sandals on his feet
Martial:	like that of Mars (the Greek Ares), god of war
brawns:	muscles
Jovial:	'Jove' is 'Jupiter' (see notes on Act II Scene 4). References to Jupiter occur throughout this play
Hecuba:	wife of Priam, King of Troy. The reference here is to her grief at the loss of her children, especially Hector, at the hands of the Greeks
main-top:	look-out platform on the main mast of a ship
pregnant:	obvious
confiners:	inhabitants
pickaxes:	Imogen here means her fingers
partisans:	long-handled spear with a broad blade

Act IV Scene 3

Bad news is coming thick and fast to Cymbeline: Imogen and Cloten have both disappeared, and the latter's absence has caused the Queen to fall ill. He threatens Pisanio with torture to make him reveal what has happened to Imogen, but Pisanio maintains that he knows nothing. The Roman legions are reported to have landed, though the British forces are said to be enough to withstand them. Pisanio, left alone, is puzzled not to have heard from either Posthumus or Imogen. He must seem dishonest to Cymbeline to keep his loyalty to them, but he determines to fight valiantly for Britain in the coming battle.

This brief scene advances the plot a little further, giving an impression of growing confusion and catastrophe for Cymbeline, but reassuring the audience, through the presence of Pisanio and the evidence of his faithfulness, that 'The heavens still must work' (lines 41)—that some providential power is in control of events.

NOTES AND GLOSSARY:
Fortune ... steer'd: sometimes boats which have lost their helmsmen may by chance find harbour

Act IV Scene 4

Guiderius hears the noise of battle near the mountain cave and is eager to join in on the British side, as is Arviragus. Belarius tries to persuade them to hide higher up the mountains, since he fears that their treatment of Cloten will bring vengeance on them, and that he himself will be recognised as an outlaw. But the young men's desire to exercise their manhood by fighting for their country proves the stronger, and so he decides to join them.

This scene underlines the natural vigour of Guiderius and Arviragus, and at the same time their unwillingness to remain in a sphere where their manliness lacks the scope for truly noble deeds. As Belarius admits in a final aside,

> ... their blood thinks scorn
> Till it fly out and show them princes born.
>
> (lines 53–4)

It is their essentially royal nature, even though they are ignorant of their birth, which spurs them on to deeds of renown. The theme is: 'Royalty will out'.

NOTES AND GLOSSARY:
importantly: with urgent business
rowel: spur

Act V Scene 1

Posthumus, who has not been seen on the stage since Act II Scene 5, now appears as one of the gentlemen enlisted in the Roman army (see Act III Scene 1). He carries in his hand 'a bloody handkerchief', the sign which Pisanio has sent him (as he commanded in a letter—see Act III Scene 4, lines 123–5) that his order for the killing of Imogen has been carried out. But Posthumus is in a very different state of mind now. He still thinks Imogen guilty of adultery, but her supposed fault seems small in comparison with his own. He decides not to fight for the Romans, but to dress as an ordinary British peasant and join Cymbeline's army.

Posthumus's repentance is sudden and unexpected, but it can be assumed that he has had time in the interval since his writing of the letter to Pisanio to regret his passionate folly. It is significant that he now has a more religious attitude; he thinks of the gods. He sees himself as more worthy of their vengeance than Imogen. Even her supposed death he sees as a sign that the gods love her, and wish to save her from greater sin. Others (and he clearly includes himself) are permitted to add one sin to another, each worse than the previous one, until the sinners repent— which he now sees as being for the sinners' ultimate good (lines 13–15). He is more patient than he was before: 'Do that which seems best to you,' he says to the gods, 'and give me the blessing of knowing how to be obedient to your will' (lines 16–17).

Posthumus's decision to fight on behalf of the British avoids the painful spectacle for the audience of seeing the hero fight against his own countrymen. It shows his basic patriotism. But it is also in tune with his changed attitude towards Imogen (see lines 19–20); in this way he is prepared to die for Imogen (lines 25–6). He will also re-affirm the earlier theme of a reality which is more than appearance by making men conscious of greater valour in him than they would expect from his lowly appearance (lines 29–30); and the scene concludes with his saying that he will start a new fashion of showing less outside and more within.

NOTES AND GLOSSARY:
wrying:	misbehaving
habits:	dress

Act V Scene 2

The Roman and British armies march over the stage in turn. The battle between them is then represented in a series of skirmishes, in one of which Posthumus (in disguise) defeats and disarms Iachimo. The Britons are put to flight, and Cymbeline is taken prisoner; but Belarius,

Guiderius and Arviragus rescue him, and rally the rest of the Britons so that flight is turned into victory. Lucius tells Imogen (dressed as his page) to flee and save herself.

This is primarily a scene of action; but Iachimo, like Posthumus in the previous scene, is also beginning to feel remorse. He has, in fact, been beaten by Posthumus, but because of the latter's disguise he thinks that it is a peasant who has defeated him. To him it seems that it is the very air of Britain which is weakening him in revenge for the wrong done to the princess of the land.

NOTES AND GLOSSARY:

Carl: churl, peasant

Or betimes / Let's reinforce or fly: let us either quickly get help or retreat

---

Act V Scene 3

Posthumus, returning from the place where he had helped to make the stand against the Romans, is asked for news by one of the British lords who had fled. He gives an account of how an old soldier (Belarius), aided by two young men (Guiderius and Arviragus), had turned British defeat into victory. He scoffs at the cowardice of the lord; but then, left to himself, resolves that since he has escaped death in the fight, he will appear once more as a Roman, and deliberately surrender himself to the Britons, in the expectation of being put to death. His grief for his treatment of Imogen is such that he no longer wishes to live. He is arrested by two British captains who immediately hand him over to Cymbeline.

This scene duplicates much of the material of Act V Scene 2. The substance of Posthumus's long speech at lines 14–51 of Scene 2 has already been shown in action in the previous scene. However, the brilliance of the narrative is such that we cannot wish Shakespeare had dispensed with it. The syntax is tortured with parentheses and interruptions, and the sense is often so compressed as to make the speech difficult to follow in detail. But the general impression is clear, and the effect of these stylistic complications is to give a very graphic rendering of a confusing battle as described by one who is excited and out of breath. It is thus a dramatic *tour de force*.

Somewhat crudely paraphrased the speech runs as follows: 'The lane was close to the battle, had ditches on either side, and was walled with turf. It gave opportunity to an old soldier (a good and reliable one, as I can testify, who for having done this for his country, deserves to be honoured for as long a time as it took him to acquire his white beard). With two youngsters—lads whom one would expect to be playing the game of "prisoner's base" rather than committing such slaughter, and whose faces were so charming they deserved to be protected by ladies' masks (or, rather, they were fairer than many faces which are masked to protect them from the elements, or for modesty's sake)—with these two the old soldier stood across the lane and blocked the passage, crying to those who fled: "Our British harts [with a pun on "hearts"] die in flight [from the hunter], not our men. Cowardly souls that run away like this fly into eternal darkness [are damned forever]! Stand! Else we will act as Romans and give you death like beasts, which you, who shun it with such bestial cowardice, may avoid if you will only turn and frown on your enemies. Stand, stand!" These three (they had the confidence, and did the work, of three thousand—for three who act become the whole troop, when all the rest do nothing) helped by the lane's situation, but even more influential because of their own nobility, which could have changed a housewife's distaff into a soldier's lance, put the colour of red gold into faces that were previously pale with terror. Some were revived by shame, some by courage, with the result that some, who had turned cowards only by imitating others (that is a sin in war, damned in those who start it) began to look the same way as the soldier and the youngsters did, and to bare their teeth like lions at the pikes of those who had been hunting them. Then the pursuers began to be checked, and a retreat was started; soon this became a rout, rapid and confused. Immediately they fled like chickens along the very same road down which they had swooped like eagles, running away like wretches where they had made strides like victors. And now our former cowards, like scraps of food in long, strenuous voyages, became the very things on which life depended. Finding that they now faced the defenceless backs of their enemies, heavens, how they struck at them! Some of them had previously pretended to be slain; some had feigned to be dying; some of them were friends who had been overtaken by the previous attack of the Romans. Previously ten Britons had been chased by one Roman; now each one of these Britons became the killer of twenty Romans. Those who were ready to die without attempting to fight are now become the deadly terrors of the battlefield.'

NOTES AND GLOSSARY:
veriest hind: merest peasant
if seconds / Had answer'd him: if others had come to give him help

Act V Scene 4

Posthumus in a British prison awaits his execution in a spirit of contrition. He falls asleep, and has a dream in which the ghosts of his father, Sicilius Leonatus, his mother, and his two brothers appear. They complain to Jupiter that Posthumus's trials have continued too long.

Jupiter then appears sitting up >n an eagle, and accompanied with thunder and lightning. He rebukes the ghosts for their impatience, but declares that Posthumus will have a happy issue out of his afflictions, and orders them to lay on Posthumus's breast a tablet which will reveal his purposes. He then disappears, and the ghosts, after carrying out his command, also make their exit. Posthumus awakes from his dream to find the tablet, in which he reads the enigmatic message that his troubles will end, and Britain be restored to peace and prosperity, when 'a lion's whelp' shall be embraced 'by a piece of tender air', and when branches which have been lopped from 'a stately cedar' are re-joined to it and made to grow again. A gaoler enters and jests with him about death, which Posthumus, however, seems to welcome as a blessed release. A messenger enters bearing an order that Posthumus's manacles are to be struck off, and he is to be brought before Cymbeline. But both Posthumus and the gaoler are still under the impression that his execution is imminent.

The penitence shown by Posthumus in Act V Scene 1 is seen to be even deeper in this scene. His readiness for death is not to be interpreted as suicidal despair, but as acceptance of what he takes to be appropriate punishment for his offence. His conscience is fettered by sin more than his body is with chains, and he prays the gods to grant him death. He uses the image of a bankrupt who is freed from further financial obligations if he pays his creditors a limited portion of what he owes them only to emphasise that for him, Posthumus, nothing less than the payment of his whole life will be sufficient (lines 18–22). And his humility (an essential sign of true repentance) is indicated by his modest comparison of his life to a coin (continuing the metaphor of paying a debt) which is lacking in solid worth itself, but is reckoned valuable because of the imprint which it bears—his coin, in particular, having value only because it is stamped with the gods' image (lines 22–6). The religious implications of this metaphor are also significant. Posthumus respects the will of the gods, representing a pagan religious power; but the connection of sin and debt would have Christian theological overtones for Shakespeare's early-seventeenth-century audience, as this was a widely known biblical manner of speaking of redemption (literally, a 'buying back' from sin).

The dream, accompanied to make it seem more grave and mystical by 'Solemn Music', and couched in a metrical form which separates it off from the rest of the play, continues this now increasingly important religious theme. The ghosts question the ways of Jupiter with men. To them it seems that the punishment which Jupiter is inflicting on Posthumus is grossly disproportionate to what an essentially good man has deserved; and they beg him to remove Posthumus's miseries, or they will complain to the rest of the gods against his injustice. Jupiter, as the throwing of his thunderbolt testifies, appears to be offended by this protest, but he is not greatly disturbed or made profoundly angry by it. His purpose transcends the understanding even of such spiritual beings as the ghosts, and much more so the understanding of ordinary mortals. Affliction is not necessarily a mark of disfavour. 'Those whom I love most I cause to suffer,' says Jupiter, 'in order to make my ultimate gift of happiness seem the more delightful for having been delayed so long' (lines 101–2). The ghosts are told that all in the end will be well with Posthumus and Imogen, and that Posthumus will be 'happier much by his affliction made' (line 108). And he confirms this with the tablet which they are told to lay on Posthumus's breast.

The tablet is a curious device. It links the seemingly unreal world of the dream with the real world of Posthumus's suffering. Posthumus, who has obviously been delighted by the dream, wakes to 'find nothing', he says (line 129); but, in fact, he discovers the tablet. The dream, then, must have greater reality than he allowed. But when he reads the message written on the tablet he finds it so puzzlingly cryptic that he can only comment that it is still a dream, or else such stuff as madmen speak without understanding—either irrational speaking, or a speech which cannot be understood by reason (lines 144–7). All this, however, is no doubt part of Jupiter's intention as well, for it helps to create a sense that here is something which goes beyond normal human understanding. The religious, not the merely rational, state of mind is needed for its meaning to be grasped.

In terms of the actual staging of this scene in Shakespeare's theatre an attempt is also made to strike wonder and amazement into the minds of the audience. Jupiter probably descends by some mechanical device from a trap-door in the roof (see above, p.12), accompanied by the rattling of 'thunder', perhaps some simple flashing effect to represent 'lightning', and even, if Sicilius's 'his celestial breath / Was sulphurous to smell' (lines 114–5) is an indication, by a special divine scent. 'The marble pavement closes' (line 120) may also point to the closing of the trap-door after Jupiter has made his re-ascent to 'heaven'. To a modern audience some of these effects might seem faintly absurd; but to those accustomed to the scenic effects which are necessary, for example, in the performance of the last act of the opera *The Magic Flute* (1791) by Wolfgang Amadeus Mozart (1756–91), the dream should present less of a problem of credibility. It is something spectacular and exciting— entertaining in its own right; and at the same time the theatrical equivalent of the change in tone and attitude can be observed in the language. Together these seem intended to arouse a sense of wonder and more-than-earthly meaning, as Shakespeare prepares his audience for the astonishing and barely credible revelations which are to come in his final scene.

NOTES AND GLOSSARY:

The penitent instrument to pick that bolt: Posthumus is locked up by his guilt; a penitential death will be the means by which he will be able to pick the lock and so free his conscience

gyves: fetters

abatement: what is left

Rates: berates

Lucina: goddess of childbirth (an attribute of Juno)

geeck: fool

Elysium: the after-world to which the blessed dead go

fangled: fond of trashy splendour

Or senseless speaking ... cannot untie: either a message which is without meaning, or a message which defies man's powers of understanding

shot: reckoning, bill

Act V Scene 5

The scene opens with the entrance of Cymbeline, accompanied by Pisanio, courtiers, and Belarius, Guiderius and Arviragus (still known only to the King as the three strangers who turned the British rout into a victory). Cymbeline honours Belarius and the two youngsters by having them stand by his side, but he regrets that the fourth unknown warrior, the common soldier who fought so valiantly (Posthumus in disguise), is not to be found. Cornelius, the Queen's physician, enters with some of the Queen's ladies to announce that the Queen has died a horrible death after making a confession of all her sins, to which the ladies were witnesses. She admitted that she had never loved Cymbeline, that she hated Imogen and would have poisoned her if Imogen had not fled the court, and that she had also intended to administer a slow poison to Cymbeline and, during the illness which would have followed, to persuade him to adopt Cloten as his successor. The Roman general, Lucius, together with Imogen, Iachimo, the soothsayer, Posthumus and other Roman prisoners, are then brought under guard to face Cymbeline. As revenge for the British lives lost in the recent battle he condemns them to death. Lucius accepts his fate stoically, but begs the life of his page (Imogen in disguise). Cymbeline is taken with the page's appearance, grants his life, and also grants any boon which the page cares to demand. Lucius (and, it would seem, Cymbeline, too) expects the page will ask for him to be pardoned, but, to his surprise and hurt, Imogen, who is disturbed by the sight of Iachimo, asks, instead, to speak privately with Cymbeline. In the meantime Belarius and the young men think that the boy resembles Fidele, and Pisanio recognises Imogen, but says nothing. After their brief conference Cymbeline calls forth Iachimo, and orders him to answer Imogen's questions. As a result, Iachimo tells, at some length, the story of the wager for the ring given to Posthumus by Imogen and the deception which he practised to make Posthumus believe that Imogen had been unfaithful. At this point Posthumus reveals himself, declares that he has procured Imogen's death, and offers himself for any torment that Cymbeline cares to inflict. As he cries out his wife's name, Imogen tries to speak to him, but, thinking that 'the page' is scorning him, Posthumus strikes Imogen and knocks her down. Pisanio is horrified, and now reveals Imogen's identity. When she recovers she turns on Pisanio and accuses him of having given her poison; but Cornelius explains how he had substituted a potion that merely induced the temporary semblance of death. Imogen and Posthumus then embrace each other, and Cymbeline and his daughter are reconciled and reunited. To add what he knows about the disappearance of Cloten, Pisanio explains how he produced a false letter which led Cloten to dress in Posthumus's clothes and pursue Imogen to Milford Haven. Guiderius then steps forward, and boldly asserts that he slew Cloten, the consequence of which is that Cymbeline is reluctantly compelled to pass the death sentence on him. This forces Belarius at last to speak out. He reveals his true identity, explains how he abducted the boys from the court, and asserts that he can prove that the two young men present are, in fact, the King's sons. Cymbeline is astonished and overjoyed; Imogen delights to find that those whom she called brothers are her brothers indeed. In this new mood of rejoicing the Roman prisoners are all pardoned. Cymbeline, however, still regrets that the brave commoner cannot be found, whereupon Posthumus reveals that it was he who fought alongside Belarius and the princes. Iachimo, conscience-stricken, now kneels before Posthumus, returns the ring and bracelet, and offers his life. Posthumus, however, forgives him; and, on that cue, Cymbeline announces that 'Pardon's the word to all'. Posthumus then asks that the Roman soothsayer be summoned to interpret the dream which came to him in his prison cell. The 'lion's whelp' is said to be Posthumus Leonatus; the 'stately cedar' is Cymbeline, the abduction of whose sons is symbolised by the lopping of branches, now re-joined to the trunk, since the King has found his sons again. Cymbeline decides that, although he is victorious, he will settle for peace, and renew the tribute to Rome, which he was originally dissuaded from paying by the wickedness of the dead Queen. This action enables the soothsayer to complete his interpretation of another dream — that of Lucius concerning the eagle vanishing into the sun. This is now seen to mean that the Roman eagle was destined to reunite with the sun of Cymbeline shining in the west. In his final speech Cymbeline ordains that the gods shall be priased and incense burnt on their altars, and that the army shall march through London with the Roman and British ensigns carried side by side in token of peace.

This scene is the great climactic moment in *Cymbeline* when tragedy is finally converted into comedy. The transformation which characterises the whole play—of misery into happiness, and wickedness into good—here reaches its supreme moment of revelation and joy. However, as if to accentuate the effect of light coming out of darkness, Shakespeare makes the scene itself repeat the tragi-comic pattern; and not once only, but three times.

Firstly, the triumph of Cymbeline's victory seems to be marred by the news of the Queen's death, but then the evidence of her confession makes it apparent what a remarkable escape Cymbeline has had from total disaster. The theme of appearance and reality, recurrent throughout the play, is also repeated in this connection. Cymbeline claims (and we are probably meant to believe him) that he was not at fault in trusting her; her 'seeming' (line 65) was such that he would have had to be totally cynical about human nature not to have had confidence in her.

Secondly, the sentence of death pronounced on the Romans seems to include Imogen, but the plea which Lucius makes on her behalf, and, even more, the impression she makes on Cymbeline (evidence of the secret sympathy of nature), brings her reprieve. Distress seems to be renewed when she fails to use her opportunity to save Lucius's life in return, and worse when Posthumus reveals himself and strikes her. Pisanio's 'How fares, my mistress' (line 236) suggests revival again, and Cymbeline exclaims:

> If this be so, the gods do mean to strike me
> To death with mortal joy.
>
> (lines 234–5)

These words aptly express the paradoxical combination of destruction and delight which characterises this whole scene. But Imogen's suspicion of Pisanio causes pain once more, only to be cancelled by Cornelius's explanation of the true properties of the potion; and secure happiness seems to be reached when Imogen, embracing Posthumus, tells him (lines 262–3) to think that he is at last on a firm rock, safe from the storm.

However, security is still not yet really achieved. Guiderius's bold assertion that he cut off Cloten's head threatens disaster again. The King is in danger of killing his eldest son. But Belarius's declaration averts this third tragic threat, and converts it into joy, which saves himself as well as Guiderius, and ultimately, the Roman prisoners, too—not excluding even the villainous, but now penitent, Iachimo. It is at this point when all has been revealed, and when all have been forgiven and all have been reconciled, that a stable and completely happy ending is reached.

The only conflict occurring within the play which remains to be resolved is that between the nation of Britain and the empire of Rome. (For a tentative explanation of the significance of this reconciliation see the comments in Part 3 below, pp.76–7.) This is effected through the almost ecstatic joy of Cymbeline, which enables him to transcend the more primitive yearning for vengeance, and assert the higher moral claim of harmony and peace in a spirit of dedication to the gods. Even such a minor detail as the calling of the soothsayer for the first time by his name, Philarmonus, contributes to this sense of a divinely sanctioned order emerging from chaos, for the soothsayer is one skilled in reading the mysterious messages of the gods. His name and office fuse with the theme of divine providence in his pronouncement that

> The fingers of the pow'rs above do tune
> The harmony of this peace.
>
> (lines 464–5)

This, together with Cymbeline's

> Laud we the gods;
> And let our crooked smokes climb to their nostrils
> From our bless'd altars
>
> (lines 474–5)

is the culmination of the sense of religious awe which has increasingly marked the tone of the play since the beginning of Act V. The actual appearance of Jupiter in Act V Scene 4 gave particular emphasis to the puzzling relationship between gods and men, but what was there left cryptic and mysterious is here illuminated as if by revelation. Despite the seemingly impossible nature of the puzzle, all the pieces are shown to fit.

Or, at least, such appears to be Shakespeare's intention. The difficulty comes with the realisation of this purpose in terms of dramatic action. Exceptionally good actors may contrive to make the alternation of threatening catastrophe and joyful harmony mount to the religious climax that is intended, but less skilful performers may well be unable to cope with some of the technical weaknesses in this scene. For example, Imogen's initial neglect of Lucius may be excused because she has more urgent business in hand, but her way of dismissing him ('... your life, good master, / Must shuffle for itself', lines 103–4) seems callously abrupt. Posthumus's striking of Imogen is an especially difficult moment to present. It is inadequately motivated and therefore apt to seem merely shocking. In addition, there is much repetition of material previously shown or narrated (in lines 179–208 and lines 326–45) which makes for tediousness and unnecessary length. Above all, the revealing of one hidden identity after another strains coincidence too far, and as a result the plot appears too obviously a contrivance for bringing all the separated characters together again in one scene and resolving their problems in the most astounding way possible. Thus, although an atmosphere of wonder is essential for the religious note on which the play is to end, the flaws in this final scene are such that wonder easily degenerates into mere sensationalism, and there is even a risk that its high seriousness will turn into absurdity.

NOTES AND GLOSSARY:

targes of proof: shields, the strength of which has been well tried

my peculiar care: what concerns me personally

straight-pight Minerva: tall and upright Minerva (the Greek Pallas Athene, a goddess of war and the handicrafts)

Phoebus' wheel: the wheel of the chariot of the sun-god, Phoebus Apollo

car: chariot

and / Throw me again: this is a loving tease—Imogen is in effect saying: 'The last thing you will want to do now is to strike me and cast me from you'

Your pleasure ... I did: my offence existed only in your willingness to believe it, I suffered punishment also because of that, and it was in your belief only that my treason existed; the only harm I did was what I suffered myself

the counterchange / Is severally in all: the exchange of joy is made between each one individually, and all are united in their mutual happiness

Philarmonus: the name means 'lover of harmony'

Leo-natus: (*Latin*) lion-born

mollis aer: (*Latin*) literally, 'tender air'

mulier: (*Latin*) literally 'wife, woman'

Lud's town: London

Part 3

Commentary

Cymbeline and the 'last plays'

Cymbeline is usually grouped with *Pericles, The Winter's Tale* and *The Tempest* as one of Shakespeare's 'last plays' or 'late romances'. The term 'tragi-comedy' is also frequently used, which could also be applied to other plays of Shakespeare, such as *Measure for Measure* and *All's Well That Ends Well*. If none of these terms is quite satisfactory, each one nevertheless tells us something which is valid about the qualities of *Cymbeline. Pericles, Cymbeline, The Winter's Tale* and *The Tempest*, probably composed in that order, belong to the final phase of Shakespeare's play-writing career, 1608–1613; and whether or not they reflect a mature, unified vision of life—the ultimate fruit of Shakespeare's intense and varied imaginative response to Elizabethan and Jacobean civilisation—it is certainly true that they have a number of features in common which give them a marked family resemblance to each other.

In each of these plays Shakespeare goes back for inspiration to the 'romances' (stories of love and adventure) which form the basis of his comedies, from *Two Gentlemen of Verona* to *As You Like It* and *Twelfth Night*. But instead of juxtaposing the world of romantic fantasy with the antithetical world of commonplace reality (summed up for us, in *A Midsummer Night's Dream*, by the image of the love-sick Queen of the Fairies wreathing her arms around an ass-headed workman) in these 'late romances' he emphasises the incredibly marvellous and exotic to the point where they seem to defy our familiar, rational view of things. At the same time painful material of the kind that seems to belong to the period of the tragedies (*c.*1599–1608) forms much of the substance of these plays. Sexual jealousy, for example, initiates a destructive movement in both *Cymbeline* and *The Winter's Tale* which seems to threaten a tragic outcome parallel to that of *Othello*; and the villainy of Iachimo, in particular, strongly resembles that of Iago. In each case, however, the outcome is finally not tragic, but comic—'comic' in the sense that the *Divina Comedia* (*c.*1300) of the Italian poet Dante Alighieri (1265–1321) is comic, that is, ending on a happy, indeed, spiritually exalted level.

Certain situations and themes likewise recur in this group of plays. As Cymbeline is divided from, but ultimately reunited with his daughter, Imogen, and his sons, Guiderius and Arviragus, so Pericles loses but finds again his daughter, Marina; Leontes (in *The Winter's Tale*) orders the death of his own child, Perdita, but at last has her restored to him; and Alonso (in *The Tempest*) thinks that his son, Ferdinand, is drowned, but ultimately finds him alive and well. Tragedy takes the form, as it did in *King Lear*, of a division between parent and child, but that division is healed, and the ending is one of reconciliation.

The estranged children may not know their own parentage—as happens with Guiderius and Arviragus—but their innate royalty shines through, nonetheless, in the generosity of their feelings and the courage and nobility of their deeds. As Belarius exclaims,

> 'Tis wonder
> That an invisible instinct should frame them
> To royalty unlearn'd, honour untaught,
> Civility not seen from other, valour
> That wildly grows in them, but yields a crop
> As if it had been sow'd.   (IV.2.177–82)

This is seen as the work of 'divine Nature' (Act IV Scene 2, line 171). Royalty places these princes and princesses at the head of the social hierarchy, but their distinction is a matter of innate qualities rather than social prestige (a point underlined in *Cymbeline* by the intrinsic worthlessness of Cloten despite his position as son of the Queen). By birthright they belong to the court, and in each of these plays it is to the court that they are finally restored; but the court is represented as a place of corruption and intrigue, of false artifice and deception, from which it is necessary to withdraw, at least for a time, to recruit new energy and vigour in the country, where honesty and naturalness thrive as they cannot in the court. But the ultimate purpose of this retreat is to inject new life into the court. The typical plot-structure is therefore circular: from court to pastoral retreat, but back to court again; and the movement from parents to children, and finally to their reunion, is accompanied with a sense of renewal and regeneration.

The gods

In all this the gods play a significant role. A masque of Iris, Ceres and Juno is presented in *The Tempest*, and Prospero (though he remains an imperfect mortal and returns at the end of the play to a limited human role) is able to act with magical powers upon his enemies, simulating through Ariel the effect of Destiny and Fate:

> You are three men of sin, whom Destiny,
> That hath to instrument this lower world
> And what it in't, the never-surfeited sea
> Hath caus'd to belch up you ...   (III.3.52–5)

In *The Winter's Tale* appeal is made to the oracle of Apollo to establish the innocence or guilt of Hermione, and when Leontes defies its message the consequences are such that Leontes himself is forced to recognise that he is being punished for his sin:

Apollo's angry; and the heavens themselves
Do strike at my injustice.   (III.2.143–4)

In *Cymbeline* Posthumus, while prisoner in a British gaol, has a vision of the spirits of his ancestors, and of the descent of Jupiter 'in thunder and lightning, sitting upon an eagle' (Act V Scene 4). References to the gods, or divine power, are frequent throughout the play, but especially so in the last act. In Act V Scene 1 Posthumus, reappearing after a lengthy absence, repents his treatment of Imogen, and shows his sorrow by offering himself to the vengeance of the gods (lines 7–11). More appropriately, he decides to accept whatever it is their will to do, and prays that they will grant him a submissive frame of mind:

Do your best wills,
And make me blest to obey.   (lines 16–17)

In Act V Scene 3 a British Captain praises Jupiter for the victory over the Romans (line 84), and in the following scene, Act V Scene 4, it is the complaint of Posthumus's ancestors against the seeming injustice of Jupiter which causes the god to come on to the stage to vindicate his ways.

Act V Scene 5, however, is the scene which most abounds in such references. Cymbeline, hearing of the Queen's confession, realises something of his own folly, and exclaims, 'Heaven mend all!' (line 68). Iachimo in his somewhat prolix account of the wager makes references to Venus and Minerva (line 164) and Diana (line 180)—unimportant in themselves, but enough, perhaps, to keep the idea of the gods in the audience's mind, as does the metaphor in Posthumus's condemnation of Iachimo as 'sacrilegious thief' stealing from Imogen's 'temple / Of virtue' (lines 220–1). More significantly, when Pisanio reveals Imogen's identity, Cymbeline expresses his joy that she is alive and beside him, with the words:

If this be so, the gods do mean to strike me
To death with mortal joy.   (lines 234–5)

And Pisanio defends himself from Imogen's charge of poisoning her with

Lady,
The gods throw stones of sulphur on me, if
That box I gave you was not thought by me
A precious thing!   (lines 239–42)

There are trivial references again in lines 243 and 287, and indirect, but slightly more meaningful, suggestions of divine sanction in Cymbeline's words to Imogen in lines 268–9 ('tears' as 'holy water' gives human grief a religious value). These are echoed in Belarius's prayer for Guiderius and Arviragus:

The benediction of these covering heavens
Fall on their heads like dew!

(lines 350–1)

A much stronger chord, however, is struck in the lines expressing Cymbeline's pleasure in the harmony at last established among all the major characters of the play:

See,
Posthumus anchors upon Imogen;
And she, like harmless lightning, throws her eye
On him, her brothers, me, her master, hitting
Each object with a joy; the counterchange
Is severally in all. Let's quit this ground,
And smoke the temple with our sacrifices.

(lines 392–8)

The image of Posthumus embracing Imogen as a ship that is now safely anchored in harbour recalls Pisanio's final speech in Act IV Scene 3. Ignorant of what has happened to Posthumus, to Imogen, and to Cloten—'Perplex'd in all'—Pisanio had yet trusted in divine providence: 'The heavens still must work' (line 41); and it is with a re-affirmation of such faith that he closes the scene: 'Fortune brings in some boats that are not steer'd'. Fortune has now brought in this particular boat; and it is seen that 'Fortune' is not just chance, but the agent of the gods. The phrase, 'like harmless lightning', applied to Imogen's loving glances at Posthumus, Guiderius, Arviragus, Cymbeline and Lucius, may also be meant to recall a previous scene—in this case, Act V Scene 4, with the descent of Jupiter accompanied by thunder and lightning. That Imogen's glance is '*harmless* lightning' suggests the transformation of divine anger into divine joy. It is a realisation of what Jupiter had claimed to be the nature of the divine order of things:

Whom best I love I cross; to make my gift,
The more delay'd, delighted.

(V.4.101–2)

All has been delayed till this last scene, but now the gift of the divine blessings is the more ecstatically received by everyone because of the crosses which have preceded it. And, in conclusion, lines 397–8 constitute an acknowledgment of the gratitude due to the gods, the 'sacrifices' clearly being happy ones betokening thanksgiving rather than propitiation.

This note of positive beneficence characterises all the remaining references to the gods in Act V Scene 5, including Philarmonus's interpretation of the message left to Posthumus in his dream-vision (lines 435–56); the soothsayer's own comment that 'The fingers of the pow'rs above do tune / The harmony of this peace' (lines 464–5); Cymbeline's repeated exhortation to sacrifice to the gods (lines 474–5); and his final assertion that the peace between Britain and Rome will be ratified 'in the temple of great Jupiter' (line 480). The gods, Jupiter in particular, are now figured as controllers and directors of events which have been bewilderingly painful hitherto (prompting mortals, with their limited understanding, and even spirits such as Posthumus's ancestors, to question divine order), but which are now seen to form part of a transcendent providence.

Problems of dramatising romance

The presence of such qualities as these—suggesting the emergence of a new and exalted order from what threatened to bring about tragic disorder—has prompted E. M. W. Tillyard, for example, in his *Shakespeare's Last Plays* (Chatto & Windus, London, 1938, pp.16–22), to compare the 'last plays' to the third play in a Greek tragic trilogy. Such a third play restores harmony after the disruption represented in the preceding plays, and reconciles conflicting parties. The 'last plays' are in this sense, sequels to Shakespeare's tragedies. The perfect working out of such a pattern is accomplished in *The Winter's Tale*; *Cymbeline* (usually regarded as slightly earlier in date) is only a partially successful attempt—a precursor of what is to follow.

The objection to this, and similar views, has been stated by J. M. Nosworthy in his Introduction to the Arden edition of *Cymbeline*. 'In general,' he says, 'these interpretations seem to me to emphasise certain aspects of the play, sometimes arbitrarily selected, at the expense of others of equal or greater importance' (p.xlv). The problem resides in the unevenness and diversity of *Cymbeline*. It is difficult to take all of the play's many facets into consideration—Shakespeare is, perhaps, asking us to hold too many things in mind at the same time; and it is equally difficult to decide whether this variableness, in both design and execution, is the result of confusion, that is, a failure of control on Shakespeare's part, or of a novelty and complexity of purpose which bewilders us only because our understanding of it is inadequate.

In the discussion of Act IV Scene 2 above, it has been suggested that the excess of coincidence and the absurd misidentification of Cloten's body in that scene are part of a skilful, rather than inept, dramaturgy which is intended 'to stifle the audience's criticism of the incredibility and absurdity of what they are seeing enacted on the stage before their eyes'. If this were a narrative 'romance', this defence would be unnecessary. Such a story, beginning with its 'Once upon a time' formula, would transport the reader (the author, be it noted, would be concerned only with a reader, not with the effect of performance on an audience) into a fantasy world of the mind, where the criteria of ordinary experience do not apply. Each reader would be free to visualise it, or not to visualise it, in more or less detail, according to his own inclinations. The scope, that is to say, for a purely subjective, imaginative response would be comparatively unrestricted. In dramatising such a story, however, and putting it upon the stage, the author narrows this capacity for subjective response. All the members of the audience hear the same words being spoken and see the same figures performing the same actions with the same degree of carefully rehearsed movement and gesture. The Elizabethan/Jacobean theatre (see above pp.12–17) employed conventions which were less realistic than those of the modern stage (and, of course, still less realistic than those of the cinema and television), and to this extent Shakespeare's task, and the task of his contemporary actors, would be less difficult than that which faces a modern producer of *Cymbeline*. But the step from narrative to dramatic 'romance', from fantasy world of the mind to the far more substantial world of the living theatre, would still be a large one, attended with many risks of absurdity.

Shakespeare had the choice of two broadly contrasting methods for solving this problem: (1) he could give immediacy to his characters and their behaviour, and arouse active sympathy on their behalf, as he had done in his mature comedies and tragedies, so that each member of the audience might feel involved in their destinies; or (2) he could distance his characters by giving them a stylised quality which would emphasise their symbolic, non-realistic function, and deliberately exaggerate the preposterousness of their actions in order to make the audience aware that the world in which such characters live, move and have their being is, like the theatre itself, essentially compounded of illusion and make-believe. Judging on the basis of the impression created by the 'last plays' as a group he seems to have opted mainly for the second method, but without entirely abandoning the first. The aim would seem to have been a happy combination of the two, but with the emphasis falling on the imaginative effects made possible by accentuating the element of illusion. In *Cymbeline*, however, the yoking of the two methods is imperfect, and the result sometimes disconcerting.

The characters

Imogen

Of the main characters in the play Imogen and Iachimo are the most psychologically convincing. Imogen, like such heroines of the comedies as Portia, Rosalind and Viola (in *The Merchant of Venice*, *As You Like It* and *Twelfth Night* respectively), is sensitively feminine, but also possesses masculine boldness and outspokenness. Like them she also adopts disguise as a boy, thus emphasising her active self-assertiveness rather than female passivity. She is reminiscent, too, of Cordelia (in *King Lear*) when she resists her father's pressure to favour Cloten instead of Posthumus, and, like Cordelia, wins strong support from the audience in her stand for truth and right values against mere flattery and unquestioning obedience. She is equally firm and clear-sighted when she foils Iachimo's attempt to gain her by lying about Posthumus (Act I Scene 6); but, less in character, she proves more susceptible to his recantation and subsequent flattery of Posthumus—a sign, perhaps, of the love that makes her vulnerable, but more probably a concession to the needs of plot, since this paves the way for Iachimo's device of the trunk.

However, Imogen's behaviour in the Welsh scenes of Acts III and IV has more to do with the play's thematic requirements than expression of her character. For example, her immediate liking for Guiderius and Arviragus, and their liking for her, shows the mutual attraction generated by innate virtue and natural royalty; it is part of the 'blood will out' theme which marks all the pastoral scenes of this play. Imogen's remarkable soliloquy in Act IV Scene 2 (lines 292–333) has already been discussed. If it were taken on a realistic level it would make nonsense of her discrimination between Posthumus and Cloten; but its purpose has more to do with the nature of illusion and the theme of appearance and reality. Her suspicion of Pisanio is also out of character, as is her abrupt dismissal of the opportunity to save Lucius with the words, 'your life, good master,/Must shuffle for itself' (V.5.104–5). These things are required by the plot, and further the sense of bewilderment and bitterness on the part of characters caught up in the action (compare Lucius's 'The boy disdains me', line 105) which is generated only to be dispelled by the sweetness of the final resolution.

Iachimo

Iachimo serves the need of the wager plot for a stage-villain, and his penitence and confession in Act V Scene 5 is more convenient than dramatically plausible. (It is anticipated in his brief soliloquy in Act V Scene 2 (lines 1–10), though there must surely be something intentionally comic in his reflection that because he has belied the princess of this country, 'the air on't / Revengingly enfeebles me'.) However, in endowing him with suppleness of wit and a tongue which can make fashionable cynicism stingingly convincing, Shakespeare goes beyond the mere requirements of the story to create a character who is a memorable portrait of a contemporary gallant immersed in the mocking scepticism so well expressed by John Donne in his more flippant poems. He is most alive when engaged in invention, as when he builds up the false contrast between the loveliness of Imogen and the debasement of Posthumus's supposed taste for Roman prostitutes (Act I Scene 6). His language here has a perverse energy which carries the very impress of the man. The astonishing speech which he utters on emerging from the trunk to view Imogen and her chamber is finer poetry, but less essentially Iachimo. His hallmark is a kind of witty corruption, a paradoxically degraded vitality.

Posthumus

Posthumus falls more awkwardly between symbol and character. As the 'poor but worthy gentleman' (Act I Scene 1, line 7) discussed by the two gentlemen in the opening scene, and the clear-eyed choice of Imogen, he is the mirror of true courtliness—brave, honourable, wise and modest. In him there is no division between appearance and reality. As the First Gentleman says,

> I do not think
> So fair an outward and such stuff within
> Endows a man but he.
>
> (I.1.22–4)

Nevertheless, the onlookers are themselves decieved a little, not by any intentional misrepresentation on Posthumus's part, but by the air of accomplishment which makes him seem more mature than he is. His knowledge of the world does not extend to an understanding of the way in which circumstantial evidence can be manipulated to create false appearance, and his knowledge of himself is defective as well. When he succumbs to Iachimo's deception it is with an alacrity which suggests that he has an unconscious urge to believe the worst. Were it not that his soliloquy in Act II Scene 5 is preposterously exaggerated, he would seem to be tragically vulnerable to the kind of idealised love which professes abhorrence of, but is secretly attracted to, its opposite extreme of sensuality and lust. It is significant, for example, that he betrays a sense of injury in the way he speaks of Imogen's restraining him from enjoying his 'lawful pleasure', and that he thinks of her chastity as something which might have aroused desire in the aged and impotent Saturn. The grossness of his language in supposing, as the antithesis to this, that Iachimo had no need to persuade, but 'Like a full-acorn'd boar' merely 'Cried "O!"' and mounted', is equally suggestive of suppressed lust, and that Posthumus attributes to Iachimo what is in his own unconscious mind.

Yet this kind of psychological speculation seems inappropriate to the manner in which Posthumus is presented throughout most of the play. It is true that in Act V he repents his sin of ordering the murder of Imogen, and that he denounces himself as worse than any of the most detested things on earth (Act V, Scene 5, lines 215–17); but he is never brought to a proper understanding of himself. The unconsciously sensual Posthumus does not coalesce with, but is merely replaced by, a slightly chastened version of the previously idealised Posthumus, and one whose inner worth has been triumphantly vindicated by his contribution to the defeat of the Romans. Thus, his essential significance remains that of a symbol of virtue independent of the outward trappings of social rank. His most glorious deed is performed when he is dressed as a common man, and it is his own words which tell us how to interpret this:

> To shame the guise o' th' world, I will begin
> The fashion—less without and more within.

> (V.1.32–3)

Cymbeline

Cymbeline, whom the audience might have expected to be a dominant figure, since the play is named after him, is merely a weak and colourless character. Under the influence of the Queen he seems unable to distinguish the true merit of Posthumus (even though the latter is his protégé) from the boorishness of Cloten, and his anger against Imogen, though related to the theme of order, comes across as little more than petulancy. His principal role should be that of decision-maker, but, when his country is being invaded, the illness of the Queen and the disappearance of Cloten are enough to reduce him to bewilderment:

> Now for the counsel of my son and queen!
> I am amaz'd with matter.

> (IV.3.27–8)

He reacts to events rather than directs them; and though he is finally disillusioned about the Queen and happily reconciled to his own offspring, this is very much the doing of 'the pow'rs above'. In all, Cymbeline is little more than a cipher required by the plot.

The Queen

The Queen, Cloten, Belarius, Guiderius and Arviragus are primarily symbolic figures. The Queen is a fairy-tale witch, though she is less a prime mover of the wicked things done in the play than she seems likely to be at the outset. She shows the traditional step-mother's enmity toward's Imogen; her main ambition is to set her son on the throne. She is angry with Imogen (though she hides this under a hypocritical cloak of friendliness) simply because Imogen refuses to fall in with her plans. It is evident from Act V Scene 5, lines 62–6 that she has beautiful features, and this, again, is of symbolic significance: reality is at odds with appearance.

Cloten

Cloten, on the other hand, can scarcely be imagined as handsome, and yet, presumably, his body must be well-formed if any plausibility is to be attached to Imogen's mistake in Act IV Scene 2. It is in his mind and manners that he is ugly. It is difficult to take him at all seriously. He is so dull-witted (scarcely capable of recognising when he is being made fun of) and such a clumsy fool that it is impossible to credit him with the ability to carry out a damagingly evil design. His pursuit of Imogen to Milford Haven ought to make the audience anxious on Imogen's behalf, but it is unlikely that anyone feels him to be much of a threat. Cloten is perhaps a precursor of Caliban (in *The Tempest*)—a representative of unregenerate natural man; but to name these two characters together is merely to show up the comparative banality of Cloten. (The patriotism of Cloten and the Queen is no index of their characters. At this point —in Act III Scene 1— they are simply British.)

Belarius, Guiderius and Arviragus

Belarius, Guiderius and Arviragus belong to the world of pastoral literature. Belarius, ungratefully rejected in the past by Cymbeline, is the disillusioned courtier who so often figures in poems on the superiority of country to court and city life. That he was formerly a soldier, and is now a hunter, rather than a shepherd, does not make him any less 'pastoral', for it is tone and attitude which mark the genre more than specific reference to sheep and shepherds. His moralising manner (exemplified in Act III Scene 3, lines 11–26) is typical, as is his contention that the natural life is 'nobler than attending for a check / Richer than doing nothing for a bribe' (lines 22–3). His world may have become limited to 'This rock and these demesnes' (line 70), but he has exchanged courtly dishonesty for 'honest freedom' and learnt religious reverence:

> ... paid
> More pious debts to heaven than in all
> The fore-end of my time.

(lines 71–3)

The very cave in which he and the youths live teaches them, by making them stoop as they go in and out, the virtue of humility, in contrast to the vanity and pride encouraged at court (lines 1–9). The presiding goddess is 'divine Nature' (Act IV Scene 2, line 171), and in Belarius's view she manifests herself in Guiderius and Arviragus whose varying moods of gentleness or violence are the human extension of her calms and storms (lines 170–7).

But Belarius's very disillusionment with court life, generated as it is by experience, makes it inevitable that he should see things differently from Guiderius and Arviragus. They do not have the same standard of comparison. They are birds who 'Have never wing'd from view o' the' nest', and consequently the 'quiet life' is to them more like 'A cell of ignorance' (Act III Scene 3, lines 27–44). They are eager to enlarge the scope of their actions, and as soon as an opportunity occurs of joining in their nation's fight against the Romans they seize it with fearlessness and joy. But this, too, is a confirmation, rather than contradiction, of their conventionally pastoral status; or, at least, it does not involve a rejection of the fundamentally pastoral idea that the life lived in close contact with nature is superior to that of the court and city, for the very zeal displayed by Guiderius and Arviragus is further evidence of that 'invisible instinct' on which Belarius had commented in Act IV Scene 2. Pastoral interludes of this kind—there are, for example, precedents in Spenser's *Faerie Queene*, Book VI, and in Shakespeare's *As You Like It*; and the same pattern is to be followed in *The Winter's Tale*—do not imply a permanent alienation from the main stream of national life. On the contrary, retreat to the country provides refreshment and renewal, which then enables new life to be injected into the decadent court. It is part of this ultimately beneficent design that such denizens of the pastoral world as Guiderius and Arviragus should be impatient with their restricted field of action, and that this impatience should lead to their re-integration with the larger world to which, it is finally revealed, they belong by birth. The supremely natural thing is for them to return whence they came; but only after being nurtured in the pure and invigorating atmosphere of their pastoral setting, and thereby being enabled to act regeneratively on the corrupt and degenerate world of the court.

Some elementary distinction is made between the characters of Guiderius and Arviragus. The elder brother, Guiderius, as befits the future heir to the throne of Britain, is somewhat more bold and virile than the more sensitive and musical Arviragus (in Act IV Scene 2 the latter proposes that they should sing Fidele's dirge, but as Guiderius is unwilling to sing, they speak it). Guiderius shows this forthrightness in his killing of Cloten (Act IV Scene 2) and his complete lack of compunction in declaring to Cymbeline what he has done (Act V Scene 5, lines 286–7). But both brothers respond with delicacy and feeling to the feminine appeal of Imogen (even when dressed as Fidele), and both are hardy hunters and show the utmost physical prowess in the fight which turns British defeat into victory. It is in such scenes as these that their natural royalty is revealed, and their primary role is jointly to display such royalty. By comparison with this symbolic function their individual distinctions are unimportant.

Caius Lucius and the Romans

The character of Caius Lucius, the Roman general, is likewise not greatly elaborated. He is courteous and dignified; gentle towards Imogen when, as Fidele, she offers her services as page; and he is firm when it is his business to express Caesar's anger at the non-payment of tribute. The significance of all this, however, is that he is the noble enemy. Rome has to be resisted, but cannot be despised; and Caius is the representative of Rome.

The relationship between Rome and Britain is an important theme in *Cymbeline*. The Queen (in a speech which is not to be regarded as an expression of her character) speaks with patriotic pride of the resistance made by Cymbeline's ancestors to attempted invasion by the Romans, and refers especially to Julius Caesar's landing (Act III Scene 1, lines 19–36). Posthumus also refers to this landing, claiming that the British are now

> .. men more order'd than when Julius Caesar
> Smil'd at their lack of skill, but found their courage
> Worthy his frowning at.
>
> (II.4.21–3)

When both of the passages are taken together they seem to imply that the British have great natural vigour which makes them fierce fighters, and that the very island in which they live is surrounded with 'terrible seas' and jagged rocks which break up the Roman ships like egg-shells, but that the Romans are worthy opponents whose discipline and superior civilisation are to be respected. The tribute paid by the British seems to be a token of this respect and its breaking off is an act of folly, creating division between the two countries, where in the natural course of events there ought to be harmony.

The Romans, of course, did, in a period later than Cymbeline's, conquer and occupy Britain—a fact of which all Shakespeare's audience would be aware; and Shakespeare had written admiringly of Roman virtues in previous plays such as *Julius Caesar, Coriolanus* and *Antony and Cleopatra*. The dignity and orderliness of the Roman Empire were also, doubtless, impressive to the Elizabethans, who were acutely aware of the dangers of disorder. Moreover, in the Elizabethan version of history, British and Romans alike were both descendants of the courteous Trojans—the Romans stemming from Aeneas, and the British from Brut. The decision to pay tribute, then, in spite of the victory gained by Cymbeline, may well reflect a recognition of the longer-term superiority of the Romans, at least with regard to order and civilisation, and the need for the natural vigour of the British descendants of Troy to be re-united with the courtesy and genius for discipline possessed by their distant cousins from Rome. If so, the resulting concord not only adds to that achieved by the re-union of Cymbeline with his offspring, and of Imogen with Posthumus, but echoes it too. For Britain, bold, vigorous and specially favoured by Nature, is analogous to the pastorally reared sons of Cymbeline, and Rome to the court from which those sons are separated for a while, but to which they must ultimately return as their true home and destined place of fulfilment. (Posthumus likewise is divided for a time from Imogen, but the Italy to which he goes is only nominally the Italy of the Roman Empire. In spirit it is more the Renaissance Italy of Niccolo Machiavelli (1469–1527), the political philosopher who, in *The Prince* (1573), gave realistic advice on how to govern a state and advocated the use of cunning and intimidation if necessary. To the Elizabethans, Machiavelli seemed an immoral cynic and 'Machiavellian' was a term of abuse. Shakespeare's Iachimo is 'Machiavellian' in this sense—more a modern scheming Italian than a Roman.)

The language of *Cymbeline*

The characters in *Cymbeline* exist on different planes, some conceived realistically (and given appropriate psychological complexity), some presented as symbolic figures whose significance is conventional and abstract. The language of the play is similarly varied. Indeed, it is to a very considerable extent the fluctuating quality of the language which alerts us to the variable nature of the characterisation. It is, for example, through the dramatic immediacy or lyrical remoteness, the pithy colloquialism or the rhetorical formality, of a character's utterances that we sense the degree of realism which is appropriate to that particular character, or to that character at a particular time and in particular circumstances.

Cloten's low language

With Cloten the relation between character and language is obvious. According to the convention, common in Shakespeare's plays, that low characters speak prose and more elevated characters speak verse, the scenes in which his coarse foolishness is most evident are in prose. He is then, in effect, a 'low' character. Act I Scene 2 and Act II Scene 1 are examples of such scenes; and the courtiers who share the dialogue with him also speak in prose. The subject-matter is degrading (the unpleasant smell of Cloten's body, for example, in Act I Scene 2, and his annoyance at being rebuked for swearing in Act II Scene 1), and the language is appropriately coarse and abusive ('A pox on't ... Every jackslave hath his bellyfull of fighting, and I must go up and down like a cock that nobody can match', Act II Scene 1, lines 18–21). In Act II Scene 3, however, he passes from prose to verse as he soliloquises on Imogen and then converses with her (line 64 et seq.). The influence of the more dignified Imogen draws him up, as it were, into her sphere; but he still shows his base character in the low language with which he abuses Posthumus:

> One bred of alms and foster'd with cold dishes,
> With scraps o' th' court
>
> (lines 114–50)

words which reflect more on the user than on the person to whom they are applied.

Iachimo's debased language

Another character who moves from prose to verse is Iachimo. The whole of Act I Scene 4 is in prose, and it is pervaded by the cynicism of Iachimo. The ring which Posthumus equates with his faith in Imogen's moral worth is treated flippantly by Iachimo as something which may be stolen, and in so doing he questions Posthumus's judgement of Imogen:

> You may wear her in title yours; but you know strange fowl light upon neighbouring ponds. Your ring may be stol'n too. So your brace of unprizable estimations, the one is but frail and the other casual; a cunning thief, or a that-way-accomplish'd courtier, would hazard the winning both of first and last.
>
> (lines 84–9)

The insinuative 'strange fowl light upon neighbouring ponds' is not easy to explain; but it certainly has unpleasant sexual overtones, and seems to imply that just as you cannot prevent strange birds from alighting on ponds near yours, so you cannot prevent someone from having sexual relations with the woman whom you regard as entirely your own. The meaning carries over into 'brace of unprizable estimations', for 'brace' (a pair) is normally applied to game birds; it has a debasing effect on the 'unprizable estimations' (inestimable value) to which it is applied. The associations of theft and gambling ('hazard') in the final part of the quotation also debase Posthumus's high value of Imogen; in particular, the brilliant phrase, 'a that-way-accomplish'd courtier' implies that it only needs a sophisticated man, who has cultivated the art of seducing women, to rob Imogen of her chastity, just as it only needs an expert thief to rob Posthumus of his ring. Such language also leads naturally to the proposed wager. The wager is, in fact, the translation into terms of action of what has already been expressed in Iachimo's language; and it is perhaps a sign of Posthumus's weakness—his readiness to succumb to the challenge of the wager, against his better judgment—that he, too, speaks in prose.

In the presence of Imogen, however, in Act I Scene 6, Iachimo speaks verse. Again she draws the lower character into her higher sphere. But Iachimo remains himself. His language is still that of insinuation and debasement, serving both the needs of plot and the needs of the man's cunning and subversive character. An example is his contrast between Imogen and the prostitutes with whom, he implies, Posthumus is consorting in Italy:

> Had I this cheek
> To bathe my lips upon; this hand, whose touch,
> Whose every touch, would force the feeler's soul
> To th' oath of loyalty; this object, which
> Takes prisoner the wild motion of mine eye,
> Fixing it only here; should I, damn'd then,
> Slaver with lips as common as the stairs
> That mount the Capitol; join gripes with hands
> Made hard with hourly falsehood—falsehood as
> With labour; then by-peeping in an eye
> Base and illustrious as the smoky light
> That's fed with stinking tallow—it were fit
> That all the plagues of hell should at one time
> Encounter such revolt.
>
> (lines 98–111)

The whole of this passage is one subtle, unwinding sentence. The sense is rarely bounded by the line-unit, but runs on from one line to the next; and full advantage is taken of the highly flexible versification typical of Shakespeare's last plays which allows considerable departure from the underlying metre of blank verse. The basic pattern is that of the iambic pentameter—ten syllables, consisting of an unstressed followed by a stressed syllable, thus: $\cup/\cup/\cup/\cup/\cup/$; but in line 102, for example, there are six stressed syllables, and stressed syllables follow each other in 'Tákes prísoner', 'wíld mótion', and 'míne éye'. The rhythms of actual speech are superimposed on the metrical unit, so that a compromise seems to have been reached between prose and verse. The result is that we receive the impression of great agility of mind, which is nonetheless controlled and subtly directed.

Three stages can, however, be perceived in the development of the sentence. In the first, 'Had I this cheek ... Fixing it only here', Iachimo seeks to flatter Imogen by suggesting that the impressions created by her physical beauty are such as to convert sensual into spiritual response. To paraphrase, he says that if he had the right to kiss her cheek, an act, as implied by the word 'bathe', which would be one of purification; if he had the right to touch her hand, mere contact with which would immediately compel him who felt it to swear loyalty to her; and if he had the right to gaze into these eyes which are so beautiful, but spiritually beautiful, that they tame the wild, animal-like quality of the onlooker's eye, preventing it from straying to look at any other creature ... (This series of 'ifs' is deliberately prolonged to make Imogen feel proud of the power she exerts, and to impress her with the rightness of Iachimo's response to that power.) And after so many 'ifs' the listener expects the main clause; but Iachimo holds off and enters his second stage with a fresh series, 'should I ... fed with stinking tallow'. This provides a sharp antithesis to the previous five lines. 'To bathe' a cheek, his earlier language for kissing, becomes 'Slaver with lips'; a 'touch' evoking loyalty becomes joining 'gripes' with hands associated with coarseness and falsehood; and gazing into Imogen's eyes becomes exchanging amorous looks with women whose eyes have the 'smoky light' of cheap candles.

Finally, in the third stage, which at last provides the main clause, 'it were fit ... Encounter such revolt', Iachimo draws his conclusion that the 'I' who, having the first set of qualities in his mistress, should nevertheless prefer the second set associated with prostitutes, would deserve the worst punishment that can be imagined for such desertion of good for evil.

Iachimo makes all this an hypothesis with regard to himself, but the audience is well aware that his insinuations are designed to prepare Imogen to receive the lie he is hatching—that Posthumus has actually behaved in such a way, and therefore deserves such punishment. The crucial thing poetically, however, is the conversion which is imagined from a spiritual beauty which restrains sensuality to a sensuality which knowingly embraces corruption rather than spiritual beauty. At this moment Iachimo claims to abhor the thought of such debasement, but it is his purpose to bring such debasement about. To this extent what he presents as a mere hypothesis, ultimately to discredit Posthumus (though we note that it fails to do so, as far as Imogen's opinion is concerned), proves a true image of his own nature. His language reveals him even when his own purpose is to deceive.

Imogen's language

Imogen's language, especially in her reaction to Iachimo's false story and to her father's differently motivated travesty of Posthumus in Act I Scene 1, is plainer and far less contorted. Insinuation in no way enters either her character or the part she has to play in the plot, and the antithesis which she offers in response is accordingly more succinct than Iachimo's:

Thou wrong'st a gentleman who is as far
From thy report as thou from honour.

(I.6.144–5)

And the frankness of her character is also seen in the plain, succinct manner of her reply to Cymbeline:

CYM.   Past grace? obedience?
IMO.   Past hope, and in despair; that way past grace.

(I.1.136–7)

Her role, however, if not her character, is more complex than that of Iachimo, and this gives a further dimension to her language. Iachimo's words when he praises the beauty of Imogen in Act II Scene 2, lines 14–23, are out of character. Their style, especially the image of the taper bowing towards Imogen as if attracted by the light of her eyes (lines 19–21), is appropriate to her, and dramatically effective, but not expressive of Iachimo himself. Certain passages spoken by Imogen are likewise seemingly inconsistent with her general characterisation, but highly significant in terms of her symbolic role in the play. It is, for example, surprising that so assertive and forthright a character as Imogen, having just spoken the words from Act I Scene 1 quoted above, should suddenly turn wistful and long for the simple life:

Would I were
A neat-herd's daughter, and my Leonatus
Our neighbour shepherd's son!

(lines 148–50)

The lines can, of course, be defended as an understandable—and probably only momentary—reaction to the beleaguered position that Imogen finds herself in at this point; but in the context of the play as a whole they clearly indicate her affinity with the natural values embodied in the pastoral scenes of Act III and IV. They are, that is to say, primarily justified by their thematic significance.

Imogen's soliloquy at the beginning of Act III Scene 6 shows an even more interesting mingling of different attitudes and styles. Her simple opening sentence, 'I see a man's life is a tedious one', is on the realistic level. She is disguised as a boy, and is thus having her first taste of masculine life, but feels the physical exhaustion of a woman. Her suspicion that the two beggars of whom she asked the way might have deliberately misled her is also, if not likely in itself, psychologically plausible; but her further reflections on the culpability of rich and poor liars are abstract and generalised, little in keeping with her previous manner of speaking or with her present exhausted condition:

> To lapse in fulness
> Is sorer than to lie for need; and falsehood
> Is worse in kings than beggars.
>
> (lines 12–14)

The same can be said of

> Plenty and peace breeds cowards; hardness ever
> Of hardiness is mother.
>
> (lines 21–2)

The neat rhetorical play on 'hardness' and 'hardiness' (hardship and boldness) makes the dramatic inappropriateness more evident. This, in fact, is the generalised moralising of Belarius, already heard by the audience in Act III Scene 3:

> Hail, thou fair heaven!
> We house i' the' rock, yet use thee not so hardly
> As prouder livers do.
>
> (lines 7–9)

> Consider,
> When you above perceive me like a crow,
> That it is place which lessens and sets off.
>
> (lines 11–13)

As Belarius says, 'To apprehend thus / Draws us a profit from all things we see' (lines 17–18). It is the morality of the pastoral. That Imogen starts to imitate it in Act III Scene 6 is indicative of her proximity to her unknown brothers, who also speak in such terms:

> All gold and silver rather turn to dirt,
> As 'tis no better reckon'd but of those
> Who worship dirty gods.
>
> (III.6.53–5)

And it is the style in which Imogen makes her admiring aside when she sees how courteously she is treated by those whom she had taken for savages (lines 81–6).

The lyrical style

When Imogen is thought to be dead the terms in which she is spoken of by Guiderius and Arviragus have the lyrical quality of Iachimo's out-of-character praise of her beauty in Act II Scene 2. Iachimo's image for her eyelids,

> these windows white and azure, lac'd
> With blue of heaven's own tinct,
>
> (lines 22–3)

is echoed in the words of Arviragus that she will not lack 'The azur'd hare-bell, like thy veins' (Act IV Scene 2, lines 223–4). The entire flower-piece from which this quotation comes (in the tradition to which Ophelia's flower-distribution belongs in *Hamlet*, Act IV Scene 5, and Perdita's in *The Winter's Tale*, Act IV Scene 4) is a digression from dramatic verse, which forwards the action, into lyricism which is beautiful, but static. (A hint of this is given, perhaps, in Guiderius's impatience: 'Prithee have done, / And do not play in wench-like words ...', Act IV Scene 2, lines 230–1.) Like the songs with which there are also connections via the imagery (compare the flower references in 'Hark, hark! the lark', Act II Scene 2, lines 19–27), such lyricism suspends the action while the audience enjoys the poetry for its own sake.

The lyrical style, however, does contribute to the total meaning of the play. For example, the purpose of Arviragus's flower-piece in Act IV is to create a mood of sadness which is also one of harmony. It leads naturally into the funeral dirge, 'Fear no more the heat o' th' sun', which again holds up the action while death is celebrated as a 'quiet consummation' rather than a searing catastrophe. Death is a leveller:

> Golden lads and girls all must,
> As chimney-sweepers, come to dust,
>
> (lines 263–4)

but also a refuge from 'the heat o' th' sun', 'the furious winter's rages' and 'the tyrant's stroke'; it is immune from both the natural afflictions of lightning and thunder and the man-made afflictions of slander and back-biting. In this way death is made to seem yet another version of the pastoral retreat, a thing to be desired rather than feared, and a comment on the dangers and corruption which attend life in the larger world outside. Moreover, it may seem a leisurely irrelevance at this moment, but when considered in the context of the play as a whole it has a curiously tragi-comic (as opposed to purely tragic) appropriateness. Fidele, after all, is not really dead; within another ten lines the audience are to see her wake up and make her preposterous misidentification of Cloten's body. In the end she is also to be reconciled to her husband and father and united with these unknown brothers who now think that they are consigning her to her grave. Such 'death' is not therefore cause for profound, inconsolable grief. The pastoral tone of the dirge is right, for Fidele is no more finally lost to Guiderius and Arviragus than they themselves are finally lost to the court from which Belarius stole them.

Images of growth

The audience know that the potion which Imogen has swallowed is not fatal, since they have already been informed by Cornelius that

> there is
> No danger in what show of death it makes,
> More than the locking up the spirits a time,
> To be more fresh, reviving.
>
> (I.5.39–42)

These, too, are words which have a resonant effect extending beyond their immediate context and relevant, ultimately, to the tragi-comic nature of the play as a whole. They belong to a net-work of images which, by keeping the theme of growth present to the audience's imagination, sustains the idea of regeneration and renewal in which the play is ultimately to find its conclusion. These images transcend the particular scenes in which they appear and may well contradict the immediate situation. An example is Iachimo's murmuring as he steps from the trunk in Act II Scene 2:

> The crickets sing, and man's o'erlabour'd sense
> Repairs itself by rest.
>
> (lines 11–12)

This scene is one in which Iachimo collects the information which is to enable him to bring destruction to Imogen and Posthumus. It is part of the play's tragic movement. But the notion of sleep as rest and renewal makes it akin to the 'show of death', followed by a revival which is 'more fresh', in Cornelius's account of the Queen's potion. In the scene in which it appears it is no more than a way of saying that all is asleep, and it will so be understood by the audience at that moment; but the suggestion of 'Repairs itself by rest' is lodged somewhere on the fringe of consciousness to give a hint of a counter-tragic force which is only fully appreciated at the end of the play.

Other examples are Act I Scene 1, line 132; Act I Scene 4, lines 36–7; Act I Scene 6, line 17 ('th' Arabian bird' = the phoenix, which is born again from its own ashes); Act II Scene IV, lines 5–6; Act III Scene 3, lines 60–4; Act IV Scene 2, lines 57–61; Act V Scene 4, lines 141–4. A particular variation occurring in several of these examples is growth as related to a tree. It is most emphatic in Belarius's account of his losing Cymbeline's favour in Act III Scene 3, lines 60–4. While Cymbeline loved him, he says, he was 'as a tree / Whose boughs did bend with fruit'. The calumny which alienated the King from him was, however, like a night storm:

But in one night
A storm, or robbery, call it what you will,
Shook down my mellow hangings, nay, my leaves,
And left me bare to weather.

The implications here are destructive and tragic; but the image also hints that the tree may grow again, and this is given positive emphasis in the message which Jupiter leaves for Posthumus in Act V Scene 4:

When as a lion's whelp shall, to himself unknown, without seeking find, and be embrac'd by a piece of tender air; and *when from a stately cedar shall be lopp'd branches which, being dead many years, shall after revive, be jointed to the old stock, and freshly grow*; then shall Posthumus end his miseries, Britain be fortunate and flourish in peace and plenty.

(lines 138–43)

The fact that when this message is interpreted by the soothsayer, Philarmonus, in Act V Scene 5, lines 451–6, the tree is taken to refer to Cymbeline, rather than Belarius, and the fallen leaves have changed to 'lopp'd branches' signifying Guiderius and Arviragus, is not damaging to the play's imaginative coherence. In Act V Scene 5, lines 263–4, the tree becomes Posthumus, and Imogen, who is embracing him, its fruit: 'Hang there like fruit, my soul, / Till the tree die!' What matters is the underlying suggestion of wintry deprivation, followed by renewed growth, and the sense that such growth is the realisation of a promise which has been implicit even in the most tragic-seeming scenes.

Tragi-comedy

We come back, then, to the concept of *Cymbeline* as a tragi-comedy, but with the realisation that this involves more than simply a movement towards tragedy which is happily converted into comedy. Even while the tragedy is developing there are contrary pressures at work which ensure that the full destructive potentiality of tragedy shall not be unleashed.

Tragi-comedy, it would be truer to say, contains tragedy rather than converts it into comedy. The gods are there to keep a watchful eye on things, and though they may take a slightly perverse pleasure in bewildering and tormenting their favourites, they do so to make their gift of ultimate happiness 'the more delay'd, delighted'. Moreover, it is the characters *within* the play, not the audience *of* the play, who suffer the bewilderment and anxiety in its most extreme form. The audience are to some extent let into the secrets of the gods; their knowledge is greater than that of the characters, so that even while they sympathise with the predicaments of Imogen or Posthumus—or Posthumus's ancestors (in Act V Scene 4)—they are in possession of facts (about the nature of the Queen's potion, for example, or the whereabouts of Imogen) which give them a more reassuring perspective on the action.

The instruments of evil, the characters who would set the tragic action in motion, are likewise less terrifying to the audience than those of tragedy proper. The Queen is a fairy-story witch rather than a convincing Lady Macbeth; Iachimo is a super-subtle Italian, but less than a ruthless Iago; Cloten is also a figure of farce. And the plane on which the action moves can shift from that of psychological probability to that pastoral convention and a static lyrical beauty which has little to do with realism. Finally, the images of growth, transcending their immediate contexts, hint at a regenerative power capable of overcoming destruction.

Hence in *Cymbeline* the sting is taken out of tragedy. Much in it is painful; but it is a pain destined to be cured. The end is joy made all the greater by virtue of what has been passed through to reach it.

Part 4

Hints for study

Methods of study

It is necessary, first of all, to establish the plot-structure of *Cymbeline* and the relationship between its parts. This can be done by turning back to pp.18–19 of these Notes and studying the general outline which is given there. A useful exercise is then to attempt a summary of the episodes which form the four strands of the plot: the Iachimo–Posthumus wager; the Queen's conspiracy; the abduction of the King's sons and their life in the Welsh mountains; and the conflict between Britain and Rome. Notice the points at which one strand becomes enmeshed with another, and see how these relationships become increasingly complex as the play nears the final scene with its elaborate series of revelations and reconciliations. A re-reading of the plot summaries at the beginning of each scene discussed in Part 2 of these Notes will help to disentangle this complex web.

Not the least of Shakespeare's achievements in *Cymbeline* is the skilful manipulation of greatly diversified material so that it forms an interconnected whole, culminating in the carefully arranged springs which, in the last scene, set off one surprising dénouement after another. But consider the difficulties which also stand in the way of this scene as it might be performed in the theatre. There is a point at which astonishment becomes sensationalism, and does Shakespeare perhaps go beyond that point?

Then there is the question of the form and tone of the play. *Cymbeline* shares its tragi-comic pattern with the other 'last plays', *Pericles, The Winter's Tale* and *The Tempest*. Read these plays as well (especially *The Winter's Tale*). Consider how in each of them a potentially tragic situation is directed in the end towards the happy conclusion of comedy ('comedy', of course, not being used in the modern sense of a play full of laughs but of one that ends happily), and study the main characters, paying particular attention to the father–child relationship of Pericles and Marina (*Pericles*), Leontes and Perdita (*The Winter's Tale*), and Prospero and Miranda (*The Tempest*). Notice that the 'tragic' parts of *Pericles* and *The Winter's Tale* are associated with division between father and child, and their 'comic' conclusions with reunion. In *The Tempest* Miranda is not separated from Prospero, but a parallel is afforded in the separation of Alonso from his son, Ferdinand, each fearing the other dead, and their ultimate reunion. In all three plays the marriage of the child (Marina to Lysimachus, Perdita to Florizel, Miranda to Ferdinand) forms part of the final harmony and promises new life and hope. The general similarity to the Cymbeline–Imogen situation, and the marriage of Imogen to Posthumus, underlines the point that in this group of 'last plays' Shakespeare is creating variations on the same theme, and to this extent what happens in one play can be used to illuminate what happens in the others.

The work of certain critics who consider these plays as a group, notably G. Wilson Knight, E. M. W. Tillyard, and E. C. Pettet (see Part 5: Suggestions for further reading), will be a further help to understanding the features they have in common, and will not only reinforce the impression that they constitute an imaginative unity, but also contribute much towards the understanding of the moral vision which seems to inform them. The tragic emphasis on death seems to be replaced with a new emphasis on life and regeneration. In the words of the old shepherd in *The Winter's Tale* who has just found the baby Perdita, spoken to his son who has just described the deaths of Antigonus and the sailors: 'Now bless thyself; thou met'st with things dying, I with things new-born' (Act IV Scene 2). Forgiveness triumphs over revenge: 'the rarer action is/In virtue than in vengeance' (Prospero in *The Tempest*, Act V Scene 1). The good are persecuted, but providence is finally asserted; as Gower says in the epilogue to *Pericles*:

> Virtue preserv'd from fell destruction's blast,
> Led on by heaven, and crown'd with joy at last.
> *(Pericles*, V.3.90–1)

And, despite temporary doubt and bewilderment, it is finally seen that

> The fingers of the pow'rs above do tune
> The harmony of this peace.
> *(Cymbeline*, V.5.464–5)

However, you will also need to ask yourself whether such an exalted mood is appropriate to these plays at all points, and whether *Cymbeline* in particular is sufficiently consistent to justify its interpretation in terms of such a profound moral vision. Various objections might be made. It might be said, for example, that the cunning of Iachimo as shown in Act I Scenes 4 and 6 is difficult to reconcile with his remorse in Act V Scene 2, and especially with his curious notion in the latter scene that:

> I have belied a lady,
> The Princess of this country, and the air on't
> Revengingly enfeebles me.
> (lines 3–4)

There seems to be a change here from the language of tragic reality to the more fanciful language of the pastoral scenes. And it might be argued that the beautiful verse of these scenes, notably the elegiac flower-piece of Arviragus (Act IV Scene 2, lines 219–30) and the dirge, 'Fear no more the heat o' th' sun' (Act IV Scene 2, lines 259–82), use charming lyricism to prettify death, with the result that its tragic significance fades into the background. The extravagances of Imogen's soliloquy a few lines after (lines 292–333) might seem yet another weird change of mood and style which makes death, this time, a subject of farce. Elsewhere, the use of a rather old-fashioned sing-song verse as the medium for Posthumus's ancestors (Act V Scene 4) might seem rather wooden language for supposedly noble characters, and Posthumus's account of the fight in the narrow lane in Act V Scene 3 might seem the very reverse of clear, straightforward narrative.

These are carping criticisms, of course, which careful reflection can dispose of adequately (some of the arguments which might be used to refute them are given in the summaries of Part 2). But they do draw attention to the variable nature of the language in which *Cymbeline* is expressed. This is something of which the reader needs to be aware. It has its counterpart in the action, too. A producer of the play could not impose a single, uniform acting style on all his actors. What would do for Iachimo would not be suitable for Guiderius, since the one is conceived as a plausibly life-like character, and the other is a symbolic figure from the world of pastoral and romance. Similarly, the staging of Act I Scene 4, with its realistic imitation of the fashionable cynicism of young gallants, would require quite different treatment from that of Act V Scene 4, where 'Jupiter descends in thunder and lightning, sitting upon an eagle'. The latter supposes a mode, like that of pantomime or opera, which is palpably unrealistic, but works precisely because it does not pretend to be real. A dream-like atmosphere has to be created (Jupiter's appearance is, after all, within the context of something dreamt by Posthumus) which the audience will agree to accept as a theatrical convention, and once this is done it can become the means by which material outside the realm of ordinary, familiar experience may be conveyed.

Because of this variety of language and theatrical presentation *Cymbeline* can be a somewhat confusing play. By strenuous effort it might perhaps be possible to argue that everything is just as it should be, and there is no lack of critics who try to suggest that Shakespeare has a marvellous, transcendent vision, which, if properly understood, will explain and justify all the apparent lapses and oddities in the play. The more sensible view, however, is that of J. M. Nosworthy, the editor of the Arden edition, who regards it as 'experimental romance'. Both *Pericles* and *Cymbeline*, he suggests, 'represent the first fruits of a new attempt and are in consequence, experimental to a high degree and prone to partial or total failure' (p.xlix). It is necessary to study the different kinds of effect which Shakespeare seems to be trying to achieve in different scenes, and through the development of different kinds of language and characterisation, and it is useful to consider, as we have done in these Notes, what may be the nature of the overall pattern into which this diversity fits; but we should not be afraid to admit that some details may not fit, and that Shakespeare has overdone certain effects, and here and there produced some which are incongruous or banal. Precisely what is regarded as successful and what is regarded as unsuccessful each student will have to decide for himself. Criticism is ultimately not a science, but a matter of personal impression. On the other hand, it is best to think carefully before condemning; and it is essential to realise that ordinary standards of versimilitude and truth-to-life are insufficient for proper judgement of a play like *Cymbeline*.

To sum up, there is no simple rule-of-thumb which can guide the student to a sure appreciation of this play. In it Shakespeare seems to have been undertaking what was even for him—a man of genius, and with great experience of writing for the theatre behind him—an unprecedently difficult task. But there are perhaps two things which are especially helpful: (1) knowledge of Elizabethan and Jacobean poetry, and (2) knowledge of Shakespeare's theatre. Some of the more cynical 'Songs and Sonets' of John Donne are a great help towards the understanding of Iachimo; and the pastoral poetry of the Elizabethans (for example, Book VI, Cantos 9 and 10 of *The Faerie Queene*) provides an invaluable aid to the interpretation of the scenes in the Welsh mountains. Equally, knowledge of Shakespeare's theatre and the nature of its conventions can help us to imagine how the rapid flow of action and the artificiality of many of the speeches in *Cymbeline* might be made to work quite successfully in his own day. The expectations of audiences, especially with regard to stage illusion, were very different then from what they are now; and Shakespeare almost certainly would not have had to overcome the strong resistance to 'unnatural' or 'unreal' behaviour which is bred in a modern novel-reading and television-viewing audience. The enjoyment of past literature always involves some effort of the historical imagination and a willingness to suspend assumptions that one takes for granted in the literature of one's own time. It is for the help they can give in making this effort (as well as the pleasure they can offer in their own right) that the reading of Elizabethan poetry and the study of the Elizabethan stage are recommended as an aid to the understanding and enjoyment of *Cymbeline*.

Sample answers

The following brief essays on different kinds of questions relating to *Cymbeline* are offered, not as ready-made answers to likely examination questions, but as examples of method and approach. They divide into two main categories: those concerned with detailed examination of particular speeches or scenes, and those which raise more general problems of character, theme and production.

In answering questions of the first sort it is advisable to begin by settling the context of the scene or passage, indicating briefly its relationship to the rest of the play, and then to follow with detailed comments on language, expression of character, argument, or dramatic effectiveness, as appropriate to the extract under discussion.

In answering more general questions it is still necessary to make exact and careful reference to the text of the play. Well-chosen quotations should be used to illuminate specific points; but it is a mistake to copy out lengthy passages for their own sake. All quotations and detailed references must be relevant to the subject which is being discussed. The old principle that each essay should have a beginning, a middle and an end is still a sound one. The introduction should make clear the purpose of the essay; the middle section should work this out in more detailed fashion (using relevant references and quotations); and the conclusion should indicate what the essay has achieved.

Finally, time is always a problem. Concentrate, therefore, on a few major points, and avoid the rambling, diffuse, repetitive essay. Although summary of context has been recommended for commentary questions, and an introductory statement of purpose for those of a more general nature, do not allow this preparatory material to get out of hand. One or two paragraphs will usually be enough. Similarly, avoid cluttering the middle with *too* much detail, and, again, confine the end to one paragraph of moderate length.

(1) Comment on the significance of the following speech, and relate it to the rest of the play.

> Great griefs, I see, med'cine the less, for Cloten
> Is quite forgot. He was a queen's son, boys;
> And though he came our enemy, remember
> He was paid for that. Though mean and mighty rotting
> Together have one dust, yet reverence—
> That angel of the world—doth make distinction
> Of place 'tween high and low. Our foe was princely;
> And though you took his life, as being our foe,
> Yet bury him as a prince.

The speaker is Belarius. In the earlier part of this scene (Act IV Scene 2) he and Guiderius and Arviragus have encountered Cloten in Posthumus's clothes, Guiderius has cut off Cloten's head, and Arviragus has discovered the seemingly dead body of Fidele (Imogen disguised as a boy). Sadness over the loss of Fidele completely outweighs concern for the death of Cloten, and the latter is temporarily ignored. It is in this sense that Belarius says that great griefs cure lesser ones. But he now reminds the 'boys' (Guiderius and Arviragus) that some respect must be paid to the body of Cloten, since he was a queen's son, and the result—of great significance in the remainder of the scene—is that his headless corpse is laid side by side with that of Fidele. Imogen, who has only been drugged, later wakes alone to discover what she takes to be Posthumus's body beside her, and thus believes that Cloten and Pisanio have together murdered her husband.

There is some apparent contradiction in Belarius's speech. He recognises that death is a leveller—humble men and great ones alike become mere dust, foreshadowing the dirge which is spoken a few lines later, with its burden that

Golden lads and girls all must
As chimney-sweepers, come to dust.

And yet he argues that social distinction, essentially worldly though it is, ought still to be maintained. At court this might be expected, but it is strangely out of keeping with the pastoral values which he himself professes and which give Guiderius and Arviragus their special quality of natural vigour and spontaneity, unsullied by the corruption and sophistication of the court. Guiderius had earlier expressed his contempt for the worthlessness of Cloten in the words, 'This Cloten was a fool, an empty purse; / There was no money in't', and the coarse stupidity of Cloten throughout the play confirms that this instinctive response is fully justified. It is all the more surprising, then, that the worthless Cloten should be given respect merely because 'He was a queen's son', and in a pastoral context which has seemed hitherto to have stood symbolically for innate worth as against mere appearance.

There is, however, another dimension to the pastoral, which makes Belarius's argument more comprehensible. These 'boys', though they do not know it, are the sons of Cymbeline. It is they, rather than Cloten, who are truly 'princely'; and Belarius himself wonders, in an earlier speech,

That an invisible instinct should frame them
To royalty unlearn'd, honour untaught.

Though Belarius teaches them to despise the ways of the court, they are destined at the end of the play to be reunited with their father and return to their true place by the throne. Innate worth and social status are thus combined, not opposed, in them. They renew, rather than demolish, the aristocratic ideal; and the preservation of respect—'That angel of the world'—is suited to what they will become, if not to what they seem to be at this moment.

It could be argued that this speech also looks forward to the end of the play in its plea for forgiveness rather than enmity. Cloten came as their enemy, says Belarius, but his death has settled that score. It might almost be said that to bury him is to bury hatred as well. The image of 'med'cine' in the first line perhaps carries a suggestion of healing, too. Both these hints, if valid, would then be minor anticipations of the peace and reconciliation which triumphs over conflict in the grand finale of *Cymbeline*.

But some of this is probably special pleading. In its immediate context Belarius's defence of social position undoubtedly has a jarring effect, and that its outcome should be the laying of Cloten's body by the side of Imogen's seems positively bizarre. The one excuse for this is that it is necessary for the plot. To make such a concession, however, is to admit that Shakespeare has not managed to achieve complete harmony between symbol and story. There is an awkward disjunction between the two, and the audience has the slightly embarrassed feeling that this speech is partly designed to bridge the gap.

(2) Compare and contrast the roles of Iachimo and the Queen as the chief perpetrators of evil in *Cymbeline*.

Shakespeare's first editors, his fellow-actors, Heminge and Condell, who edited the Folio of 1623, classified *Cymbeline* as a tragedy. This is clearly unsatisfactory, but it is possible to see what may have led Heminge and Condell to their decision, for there is much in the play—including suffering of the innocent, attempted rape and murder, conspiracy to gain the crown of Britain, and war—which is of an essentially tragic nature. Moreover, this tragic action is instigated by two characters, the Queen and Iachimo, who, like other perpetrators of evil in Shakespearean tragedy such as Lady Macbeth and Iago, work by falsehood and deception. Evil with them is a form of corruption hiding beneath an appearance of honesty.

Of the two it is the Queen who engages in the more obviously dangerous activities. At the beginning of the play she has already succeeded in driving a wedge between Cymbeline and his daughter, Imogen—though, characteristically, she keeps up the pretence of being a peace-maker between them; and it is undoubtedly her influence which has secured the banishment of Posthumus. Further wickedness is seen in her attempt to procure poison and in the sly means by which she passes this off to Pisanio as a cordial drug. However, the full extent of her evil designs is not revealed until her death-bed confession, reported by Cornelius in Act V Scene 5, when it emerges that she had intended to poison Imogen and use a drug on Cymbeline which would have killed him by a slow, lingering death, and during that time she would have continued her show of love to him so that he would leave the crown to Cloten. The skilful duplicity of all this is emphasised in Cymbeline's comment:

> Mine eyes
> Were not in fault, for she was beautiful;
> Mine ears, that heard her flattery; nor my heart,
> That thought her like her seeming. It had been vicious
> To have mistrusted her.
>
> (V.5.62–6)

The division between Rome and Britain, and the resulting war, seem also to have been her work, for, as we learn at the very end of the play, it was she who dissuaded Cymbeline from paying the accustomed tribute.

Iachimo's evil works mainly on Posthumus and Imogen. Its operation by deception is illustrated by his success in convincing Posthumus, on the basis of cunningly contrived circumstantial evidence, that Imogen has been false to him. His first attempt to deceive Imogen, by lying about Posthumus's behaviour in Rome, is a failure, but this is a tribute to Imogen's absolute faith in her husband. However, he nimbly resorts to a second trick (the device of the trunk), and this is successful. The consequences of his duplicity are the subverting of what had seemed a relationship of perfect mutual trust, and the exposure of Imogen to the double threat of rape by Cloten and murder on the orders of her own dearly beloved husband. Thus, though not so widespread as the Queen's, Iachimo's evil is devastating enough, and it threatens most the character who is the play's central image of virtue.

Yet neither the Queen's threats nor Iachimo's are finally realised. Not only is tragedy averted and the play concluded on a note of joy and reconciliation, but throughout there is a sense that the full tragic horror has been abated. The Queen's 'poison' is, in fact, a harmless drug substituted by Cornelius who distrusts her 'malice'. Its effect is, if anything, restorative rather than destructive:

> there is
> No danger in what show of death it makes,
> More than the locking up the spirits a time,
> To be more fresh, reviving.
>
> (I.5.39–42)

And her very character, a combination of the wicked step-mother and fairy-tale witch, tends to remove her to the world of romance where the sting of truly tragic evil has been drawn.

Iachimo is more realistically conceived. He speaks in the cynical manner of a contemporary Jacobean gallant, and the quickness of his 'Italian brain' working in the 'duller Britain' is capable of operating 'most vilely' (Act V Scene 5, lines 196–8). To this extent he is a powerful and convincing agent of evil. But, like the Queen, he fades from the scene when his initial work is done; and though he reappears in Act V Scene 2 among the Roman invaders, it is as a rather flat, symbolic figure of remorse, no longer as the lively, convincing character that he was previously. He is vanquished and disarmed by the disguised Posthumus, and comments, as one could hardly imagine the earlier Iachimo doing,

> The heaviness and guilt within my bosom
> Takes off my manhood. I have belied a lady,
> The Princess of this country, and the air on't
> Revengingly enfeebles me ...
>
> (V.2.1–4)

And in Act V Scene 5 his long, and slightly tedious, confession (stretching over lines 141–208) parallels the report of the Queen's in lines 37–61—the two together constituting a revelation of the hidden wickedness at work in the play which is more convenient for the triumph of good than absolutely convincing.

The Queen and Iachimo are thus effective, and well differentiated, instigators of evil in *Cymbeline*, but it must be admitted that they are not essentially tragic villains. Their full tragic potential is deliberately limited so that the play can achieve its tragi-comic conclusion. Heminge and Condell had the choice of only three categories—comedy, history and tragedy. If they had had a fourth, tragi-comedy, that, no doubt, is where they would have placed *Cymbeline*.

(3) Illustrate the great variety to be found in *Cymbeline*, attending especially to the variety of poetic effect.

Cymbeline is a play which has an extraordinarily rich diversity of settings, ranging from full court scenes such as those in which the British King holds audience with the Roman ambassador (Act III Scenes 1 and 5), through the privacy and intimacy of Imogen's bedchamber (Act II Scene 2) and the fresh open-air scenes in the Welsh mountains (Act III Scenes 3 and 6, Act IV Scenes 2 and 4), and to the remarkable scene (Act V Scene 4) which not only presents Posthumus in his dark prison, but also the vision of his ancestors and the descent of Jupiter 'in thunder and lightning, sitting upon an eagle'. The characters are equally diversified: they include the formally splendid monarch, Cymbeline, weakly, however, subjected to the influence of his queen, who is more a wicked witch figure than a realistically conceived character; the brave, out-spoken, but very feminine Imogen (who has, as it were, a subsidiary role when disguised as the boy, Fidele); the conventionally noble hero, Posthumus; the spontaneously vigorous sons of Cymbeline, Guiderius and Arviragus (symbolic characters from the world of pastoral litera-ture); the cynical gallant, Iachimo; the crudely farcical Cloten; and the faithful servant, Pisanio.

In action, too, it is a play of variety and contrasts. In one scene alone, Act IV Scene 2, we are given the exchange of natural courtesies between Imogen and Belarius, Guiderius and Arviragus, followed by the entry of the churlish Cloten, the fight between him and Guiderius, and the garish re-entry of Guiderius bearing Cloten's head. This is contrastingly balanced by the re-entry, about a hundred lines later, of Arviragus bearing the seemingly dead body of Imogen in his arms and the tenderness with which the death of the 'boy' is reported. Next comes the purely lyric interlude of the beautiful dirge, 'Fear no more the heat o' th' sun', and the laying of the headless body of Cloten beside that of Fidele. Imogen's reaction when waking up and finding what she takes to be the body of her husband is an astonishing piece of theatrical sensation, catching the audience between sympathy for Imogen in her extreme anguish and a sense of the utter absurdity of the illusion with which she is afflicted. Finally, the scene is rounded off with the appearance of Lucius and his kindliness to the supposed boy whom he accepts as his page. Gentleness, violence, extravagant illusion and gentleness once more—it is a remarkable and characteristically tragi-comic sequence, concentrat-ing into one scene the pattern on which the whole play is based.

Shakespeare's poetic resources are likewise stretched to their utmost to accommodate this astonishing variety. The norm of the play is a very flexible blank verse. The underlying structure is a ten-syllabled line consisting of alternating unstressed and stressed syllables ($\cup / \cup / \cup / \cup / \cup /$), but hardly a line conforms exactly to this formula. The movement of the verse follows much more the natural rhythms of speech, as at the beginning of Imogen's soliloquy just referred to:

Yes, sir, to Milford Haven. Which is the way?
I thank you. By yond bush? Pray, how far thither?

Each line has eleven rather than ten syllables (though 'Haven' might be pronounced as a monosyllable—'Hav'n'); in the first line the accent falls on 'Yes' rather than 'sir', and 'Which' rather than 'is', and in the second 'yond bush' are both stressed syllables. In such verse the meaning also frequently cuts across the line endings to produce a run-on, rather than end-stopped, effect, as in the following passage taken from a later part of Imogen's soliloquy:

The drug he gave me, which he said was precious
And cordial to me, have I not found it
Murd'rous to th' senses? That confirms it home.

The natural pauses come after 'gave me', 'to me' and 'to th' senses'
rather than after 'precious' and 'found it'.

The uses to which this flexible blank verse is put are, however, very
different. In Posthumus's account of the battle between the Britons and
the Romans (Act V Scene 2 lines 14–51) it becomes a highly dramatic
medium. Its bewildering parentheses, tortured syntax and compressed,
elliptical phrasing make it difficult to follow, but express the surprising
changes in the fortunes of war very effectively, and they are appropriate
to the confusion and excitement of Posthumus himself who has come
straight from the fighting. When Iachimo (in Act I Scene 6) pretends to
be astonished that Posthumus has abandoned such beauty and purity as
Imogen's for the lascivious pleasure of whoring, the verse becomes
supple enough to convey both extremes—the delicacy of Imogen's hand
'Whose every touch would force the feeler's soul / To th' oath of loyalty'
(lines 100–1), and the disgusting opposite of Posthumus's supposed

    by-peeping in an eye
Base and illustrious as the smoky light
That's fed with stinking tallow.
                                        (lines 107–9)

As used by Belarius in the pastoral scenes, it is different again, becoming
the medium for picturesque moralising:

    The gates of monarchs
Are arch'd so high that giants may jet through
And keep their impious turbans on without
Good morrow to the sun.
                                        (III.3.4–7)

This seems to transport the reader to the world of Spenser's *The Faerie
Queene*.

Other verse-forms are also used. The song, 'Hark, hark! the lark',
which Cloten uses to serenade Imogen in Act II Scene 3, is a short lyric of
alternating eight-syllabled lines, which rhyme ABABCBCB. The A and
C rhymes are, however, so closely related (sings/springs, begin/bin) that
the song seems to chime throughout with just two rhyme sounds. This
causes it to stand out from its surrounding context (which is in prose),
and, with the further help of its charmingly conventional imagery—of,
for example, the lark singing at heaven's gate, Phoebus Apollo, the god
of the sun, beginning to arise, and personified flowers opening their
eyes—it forms a marked contrast to the banality and insensitivity of
Cloten.

A more delicate distinction is made between the lyrical form of 'Fear no more the heat o' th' sun' and the context in which it appears (Act IV Scene 2). It completes, rather than contrasts with, the preceding elegiac tenderness over Fidele's death. Its basically four-stressed line has a trochaic rhythm (/ ∪), which subtly reverses the iambic rhythm (∪ /) underlying the surrounding blank verse, and its iterative structure ('Fear no more . . .', 'Fear no more . . .', 'Care no more . . .') and refrain—which causes the words 'must' and 'dust' to echo through the first three stanzas—give it an incantatory formality which heightens the funeral tone of this part of the scene. At the same time its double theme (resignation to the fact of mortality and deep delight in the release which death brings from tyranny, violence and suffering, culminating in the final couplet, 'Quiet consummation have,/And renowned by thy grave!') implies a meaning which is ultimately harmonious and fulfilling rather than tragic.

Such a purpose is more obviously behind the somewhat archaic-sounding, sing-song verse in which the apparitions of Act V Scene 4 are made to speak, and in the curiously rhymed iambic pentameters of Jupiter (they actually rhyme as quatrains for twelve lines— ABABCDCDEFEF—after which the pattern becomes GHGHGIGII). The burden of Posthumus's ancestral ghosts is a protest against what appears to be injustice on Jupiter's part in afflicting the noble Posthumus with punishments out of all proportion to his offence. Jupiter's reply is a rebuke to them for doubting his divine beneficence, and an assertion that

> Whom best I love I cross; to make my gift,
> The more delay'd, delighted.

(lines 101–2)

This is clearly a philosophical message—even, perhaps, a kind of divine revelation—which transcends the level on which the rest of the play's action is performed. It is an attempt to show that events which seem disjointed and chaotic on the natural level ('nature's law' and 'Great Nature' are emphasised in the apparitions' protest) are part of a hidden harmony belonging to the supernatural level. As such, it requires to be expressed in a mode which is quite distinct from that of the rest of *Cymbeline*—something which is neither part of the play's blank verse norm, nor capable of being equated with the songs (though having a subtle relationship with 'Fear no more the heat o' th' sun'). Shakespeare, therefore, seems to have chosen a form which, without being song-like, is remote from ordinary speech and incapable of being merged with that of the human characters. The verse of the apparitions and Jupiter satisfies this requirement, though it remains unfortunate that the supernatural voice should sound so disappointingly banal.

Jupiter's purpose is to reassure the audience that order prevails in spite of appearances to the contrary. What seems scattered and diverse is drawn by him into harmony. In endowing *Cymbeline* with so much variety of setting, character, action and poetry Shakespeare may be said to have performed the role of artistic Jupiter, for he, too, creates an impression of almost bewildering diversity and conflict which is finally seen po be part of an ordered design. At least that would appear to have been his intention. Not everything does work out perfectly, but the extent to which he succeeds is remarkable, and the variety he achieves is delightful.

Practice questions

The following are some additional questions, based on material covered in various places in these Notes, which students will find it useful to think about, and on which they might practise writing answers along the lines suggested by the above sections on 'Methods of study' and 'Sample answers'.

(1) Suggest how the 'study' and the platform stage might have been used in a Jacobean production of *Cymbeline*.

(2) What difficulties would a modern producer of *Cymbeline* be likely to encounter, and how might he overcome these difficulties?

(3) 'Pisanio is not an important character in his own right, but he serves as a useful connecting link between several of the major characters.' Discuss.

(4) 'In Imogen, Guiderius and Arviragus one sees children who reveal aspects of the royalty which their father, Cymbeline, ought to embody, but does not. In Cloten one sees a child who reveals the hidden foulness of his mother, the Queen.' In the light of this comment discuss the relationship between Cymbeline and his children, and the Queen and her son.

(5) Discuss the way in which the conflict between Britain and Rome is presented.

(6) Illustrate the use of the soliloquy in *Cymbeline*.

(7) Explain the meaning of 'pastoral' as applied to the scenes in the Welsh mountains. What is the relationship between these scenes and the rest of the play?

(8) Comment on the language and themes of one of the following passages, and show its connection with the rest of the play: Act I Scene 1, lines 131–50 ('Past grace? obedience? ... Our neighbour shepherd's son!'); Act II Scene 2, lines 11–51 ('The crickets sing ... Time, time!'); Act III Scene 3, lines 79–107 ('How hard it is to hide the sparks of nature! ... The game is up.'); Act V Scene 5, lines 425–83 ('Good my lord of Rome ... with such a peace').

(9) Write on one of the following themes in *Cymbeline*: nature; the gods; appearance and reality; death; honour.

(10) 'The saying that "the spectator sees most of the game" is given new meaning by *Cymbeline*. The difference between the characters' limited view of events within the play and the audience's greater understanding, from outside the play, is of considerable importance.' Discuss.

(11) 'The final scene of *Cymbeline* is a masterpiece of construction. There all the play's knots are skilfully untied.' 'The final scene is preposterous. The audience begin to wonder what even greater absurdity will come next.' With which of these views are you more inclined to sympathise?

(12) What features does *Cymbeline* have in common with the other 'last plays'?

Part 5

Suggestions for further reading

The text

The text used throughout these Notes, and recommended to students particularly because it includes the rest of Shakespeare's plays and poems, is *William Shakespeare, The Complete Works*, edited by Peter Alexander, Collins, London and Glasgow, 1951. The best annotated text for detailed study is *Cymbeline*, edited by J. M. Nosworthy (the Arden Edition of the Works of Shakespeare), Methuen, London, 1955. Nosworthy's Introduction contains excellent comments on text, date and sources, and surveys earlier criticism, as well as offering an interesting interpretation of *Cymbeline* as 'experimental romance'. *Cymbeline*, edited by Richard Hosley (the Signet Classic Shakespeare), New American Library, New York, 1968, is a very useful working edition for the student. Besides an Introduction by the editor it includes extracts from Holinshed and Boccaccio and reprints extracts from Northrop Frye's *A Natural Perspective: The Development of Shakespearean Comedy and Romance* (1965) and Bertrand Evans's *Shakespeare's Comedies* (1960). Further reference may also be made to J. C. Maxwell's edition, *The New Cambridge Shakespeare*, Cambridge University Press, Cambridge, 1960, which has a level-headed Introduction and an informative 'Stage-History of *Cymbeline*'.

Critical, biographical and background studies

ADAMS, J. C.: *The Globe Playhouse, Its Design and Equipment*, Harvard University Press, Harvard, 1943. Useful for reference on details of Shakespeare's Globe theatre.

BULLOUGH, GEOFFREY: *Narrative and Dramatic Sources of Shakespeare*, vol. 8, Routledge & Kegan Paul, London, 1975. The most comprehensive collection of possible sources of *Cymbeline*.

CHAMBERS, E. K.: *A Short Life of Shakespeare*, Oxford University Press, Oxford, 1933. This convenient abridgement by Charles Williams of the two-volume *William Shakespeare: A Study of Facts and Problems* by E. K. Chambers gives information on Shakespeare's life and the company of actors with which he was associated, and reprints contemporary records and allusions.

HALLIDAY, F. E.: *Shakespeare in His Age*, Gerald Duckworth, London, 1956. This sketches the historical and cultural (including theatrical) background to Shakespeare's life and work.

HARTWIG, JOAN: *Shakespeare's Tragicomic Vision*, Louisiana State University Press, Baton Rouge, 1972. A very sophisticated discussion of the tragi-comic mode. Chapter III is devoted to *Cymbeline*.

KNIGHT, G. WILSON: *The Crown of Life*, Methuen, London, 1947. This studies each of the last plays, working closely on the text. The section on *Cymbeline* especially emphasises the theme of Britain and Rome.

MUIR, KENNETH: *Shakespeare's Sources*, vol. 1, Comedies and Tragedies, Methuen, London, 1957. This succinctly summarises and discusses the different sources from which the complex plot of *Cymbeline* is derived.

PETTET, E. C.: *Shakespeare and the Romance Tradition*, Staples Press, London, 1949. This is mainly useful for its clear and informative demonstration of the relationship between the last plays and earlier romance literature.

TILLYARD, E. M. W.: *Shakespeare's Last Plays*, Chatto and Windus, London, 1938. This places *Cymbeline* in the context of the post-tragic, regeneration theme which Tillyard finds in the last plays, though *Cymbeline* is seen as an imperfect expression of this theme.

WILSON, JOHN DOVER (ED.): *Life in Shakespeare's England*, Cambridge University Press, Cambridge, 1911, reprinted Penguin Books, Harmondsworth, 1944. An anthology of Elizabethan writings chosen to illustrate life in Shakespeare's age.

The author of these notes

R. P. DRAPER, who is Professor of English at the University of Aberdeen, was educated at the University of Nottingham. He has held lectureships at the University of Adelaide, South Australia, and at the University of Leicester. His publications include: *D. H. Lawrence* (1964); *D. H. Lawrence* (Profiles Series, 1969); and *D. H. Lawrence: The Critical Heritage* (1970). He has also edited Hardy, *The Tragic Novels* (1975) and George Eliot, *The Mill on the Floss* and *Silas Marner* (1977); his book on *Tragedy* is forthcoming.